# make your own
## mosaics

ANCIENT TECHNIQUES TO
CONTEMPORARY ART

For my boys

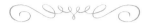

# make your own
## mosaics

### ANCIENT TECHNIQUES TO
### CONTEMPORARY ART

## HELEN MILES

## WHITE OWL
AN IMPRINT OF PEN & SWORD BOOKS LTD.
YORKSHIRE – PHILADELPHIA

First published in Great Britain in 2023 by
Pen & Sword WHITE OWL
An imprint of
Pen & Sword Books Ltd
Yorkshire – Philadelphia

ISBN 9781399006354

Printed and bound in India by Replika Press Pvt. Ltd.

Photography by Helen Miles
Design: Paul Wilkinson

Pen & Sword Books Limited incorporates the imprints of Atlas, Archaeology,
Aviation, Discovery, Family History, Fiction, History, Maritime, Military, Military
Classics, Politics, Select, Transport, True Crime, Air World, Frontline Publishing,
Leo Cooper, Remember When, Seaforth Publishing, The Praetorian Press,
Wharncliffe Local History, Wharncliffe Transport, Wharncliffe True Crime and
White Owl.

For a complete list of Pen & Sword titles please contact:
PEN & SWORD BOOKS LIMITED
47 Church Street, Barnsley, South Yorkshire, S70 2AS, England
E-mail: enquiries@pen-and-sword.co.uk
Website: www.pen-and-sword.co.uk

Or
PEN AND SWORD BOOKS
1950 Lawrence Rd, Havertown, PA 19083, USA
E-mail: Uspen-and-sword@casematepublishers.com
Website: www.penandswordbooks.com

# CONTENTS

CHAPTER 1:

# INTRODUCTION

ONE OF THE JOYS of mosaics is that they are accessible to all. If you have ever picked up a shell on the beach, been reluctant to throw away a broken bowl, or looked at a dull concrete wall and wanted to cheer it up – then mosaics are for you.

The urge to collect, gather, re-use and decorate is fundamental to the nature of mosaics. The art can require great skill and concentration, but equally, it can be applied by those with no formal training. The basic materials needed to make mosaics are not hard to come by and are often free.

The only real requirement for making mosaics is time. Mosaics cannot be rushed, and the slowness of the making process is fundamental to what they are. Mosaic-making is an art and craft which is enormously absorbing and deeply meditative. Each piece is selected and laid with deliberation and even new students mention how relaxing it is. The concentration required means that everything else around you disappears while you focus on the project in hand.

**Never miss an opportunity to collect sea worn glass, ceramic and pebbles if permitted.**

Detail from a pebble mosaic floor of a lion hunt. House of Dionysos, Archaeological Museum, Pella, Greece. Fourth century BCE.

I would argue that making mosaics is something deeply rooted and almost instinctive. Since black and white ceramic cones were pressed into plaster to create geometric designs in the city of Ur in ancient Mesopotamia 5,000 years ago, we have been making patterns and images by arranging individual pieces of things in a slow, careful and permanent way.

The people of ancient Mexico took shards of turquoise and used them to adorn human skulls, weapons and ornaments, fixing them with resin. The ancient Greeks turned the practice into a consistent art form around the fifth century BCE when

Central panel of a floor mosaic of a cat and ducks. Palazzo Massimo, Rome. First century BCE.

Representation of Spring, detail from the Triumph of Neptune, Bardo Museum, Tunisia. Late second century CE.

they started to use natural stones set into a bed of mortar to create decorative effects. The stones were sorted according to colour and size, and strips of lead were sometimes added to delineate the curve of a muscle or to separate a figure from the background.

Over time, the art of mosaic grew more sophisticated. Stone, faience, glass and ceramic were purposely cut to create mosaic tesserae, giving the makers more versatility and depth to their designs. During the height of the Hellenistic period around the second century BCE, extremely fine mosaics were made using tesserae as small as one millimetre in diameter, sometimes deliberately imitating known paintings. These mosaics were highly prized, and archaeologists have established that they were often moved from their original locations and re-embedded in new settings, indicating that their ancient owners recognised their beauty and worth.

However, it was when the Romans adopted and adapted the use of mosaics that the art spread, reaching to the furthest outposts of the vast empire. Private villas, public baths, palaces, shops and municipal buildings were all decorated with elaborate mosaics, mostly made of tessellated stone and marble. Common patterns and themes are repeated: the heads of gods and goddesses; personifications of the seasons; mythical and hunting scenes; the abundance of nature, particularly the sea; and gladiatorial battles.

That does not mean that Roman mosaics are staid, conformist or repetitive. Look closely and they will often surprise you with unexpected details – maybe a cricket hiding in an agapanthus leaf or the glitter of glass in a bird's wing – and there are many which defy expectations, showing great originality, humour and an eye for design.

One of my favourites is the theme of the 'Unswept Floor' which turns up in four different

**Money or flour bag mosaic, detail from a larger mosaic broken up in the nineteenth century. Chicago Art Institute, USA. Second century CE.**

**Swan and dolphin floor mosaic design, House of Dolphins. El Jem Museum, Tunisia. Third century CE.**

**Unswept Floor Mosaic, detail. Gregoriano Profano Museum, Vatican, Rome. Second century CE.** Photo: Alf van Beem, Wikicommons

mosaics in antiquity and features debris which has been discarded from a feast. One version can be found at the Vatican Museum and dates from the second century CE. It includes fish bones, seed pods, shells and a little mouse which has come in from a corner to nibble on a walnut.

**Saints and celestial architecture, Rotunda, Thessaloniki, Greece. Fifth century CE.**

Then something happened. As the Christian church began to take hold and its power and influence spread, mosaics began to be used in different ways. Instead of appearing in domestic and private settings, they were lifted, figuratively and literally, from floors and used as wall decorations. The Romans also used mosaics on walls but most of them were destroyed by natural disaster or invading forces and so they exist only as a footnote in the story of mosaics. From the late fourth and early fifth centuries CE onwards, mosaics were adopted by the newly expanding church to decorate their interiors. When resources allowed, everyday materials were replaced by smalti – colourful, rich, light-reflecting glass.

For the following 1,000 years, the church used its wealth to exert a semi-monopoly over mosaics, employing them to engender awe, assert power and maintain control. Living in our world of image overload, easy travel and screen entertainment, it is almost impossible to recapture the impact these mosaics must have had when they were made. Medieval worshippers accustomed to smoky, dark interiors, with no access to books, whose lives were circumscribed by the physicality of daily life, would have been almost assaulted by the mosaics: soaring basilica ceilings glittering with gold, the images of emperors and their consorts towering over their heads, sparkling surfaces rippling with colour and hinting at a tantalisingly out of reach paradise.

Combined, Roman and Byzantine mosaics span almost two millennia and offer more than enough to keep mosaic lovers happy. However, the story of mosaics does not end

**Christ the Pantocrator, Church of the Holy Saviour in Chora, (now Kariye Mosque) Istanbul, Turkey. Fourteenth century CE.**

'Folly' by Boris Anrep. Foyer of the
National Gallery, London, UK.

there. As the Byzantine empire split and
its influence waned, so too did the use
of mosaics. There is a break for a few
hundred years during which mosaics
lose their status to painting and then,
from the beginning of the nineteenth
century onwards, they are adapted and
reimagined. Mosaics as a decorative
tradition find new vigour and support
in Europe and beyond, breaking free of
the centuries-old association with the
church, and artists start using them in
original, exciting ways.

From then on mosaics have become
part of our daily landscape, adorning the
floors and ceilings of some of our finest
municipal buildings and decorating
the shop fronts of countless small-time

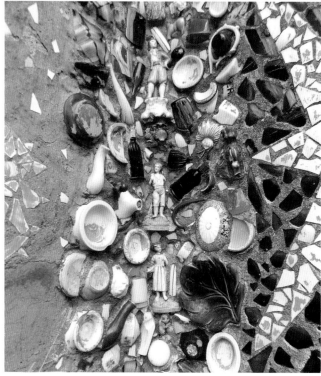

Detail from Raymond Isidore's La Maison
Picassiette, Chartres, France.

**Monument to Freedom in Kocani,
Northern Macedonia, by Gligor Cemerski.**

Photo: Raso, Wikicommons

businesses. Artists such as Diego Rivera, Marc Chagall, Picasso, Fernand Leger and Jackson Pollock experimented with the media. The Arts and Crafts Movement supported and encouraged it, and muralists, artists and crafts people have been using it in ways so varied ever since that they defy easy classification.

The use of mosaics is not culturally specific nor confined to one region. There are flourishing members' associations across the globe including in Australia, America and Europe. Schools and workshops in parts of the Middle East including Jordan and Tunisia make stunning copies and interpretations of ancient mosaics from the region along with other work. Eastern European countries which once belonged to the Soviet bloc retain vast mosaic propaganda murals.

Russia has had a history in mosaic since the founding of the Russian Imperial Manufactory in Venice and later St Petersburg, and continues to produce mosaic art, including fine examples in the Moscow Metro. A large-scale outdoor mosaic project in Chile run by Isidora Paz Lopez has transformed a grim transport hub into a dazzling display of larger-than-life renditions of local fauna and flora. The subways of New York and other American cities include examples of world-class mosaics. Commercial organisations and public bodies continue to commission new work and community groups are committed to the

**Wolf detail from the Hackney Downs Mosaic made by The Hackney Mosaic Project, a community group based in London, UK.**

craft as a way to bring people together and work on a shared outcome.

In addition, there are mosaics made by enthusiasts and professionals for private spaces and personal uses. From mirror frames to boxes, panels, stepping stones, jewellery, large wall panels, small plaques, floors, mosaicked furniture, sculptures, fire places, splashbacks and birdbaths, the possibilities are almost endless.

**Blue and green glass mosaic bird bath with fish and mirror details. Helen Miles.**

CHAPTER 2:

# GETTING STARTED

THE MOST IMPORTANT thing if you have an urge to make mosaics is to respond to that urge and get started. Join Facebook and other online groups, follow your favourite artists, comment, ask questions, and engage with other people with the same interests. Better yet, subscribe to a dedicated mosaic community – such as the Society of American Mosaic Artists (SAMA) in the US or the British Association for Modern Mosaics (BAMM) in the UK. Organisations like these offer support, information, and the chance to exhibit as well as free skill shares and other learning opportunities.

It would be ideal to have a dedicated room or studio packed with specialised tools and materials, but it is also perfectly possible to work at the kitchen table when the breakfast things have been cleared away using materials that you have collected.

Natural light, a water tap, and an outdoor space are desirable, but I have made mosaics in a window-less garage using the kitchen sink so do not allow logistical difficulties to stand in your way.

The key thing to bear in mind, however, is that the process is messy. Dust, shards, and broken tiles are an evitable by-product and so it is advisable to work in a room with a floor that can be swept. It is also important to observe some basic health and safety rules, wearing a dust mask and/or safety glasses when needed, and keeping sharp tools out of reach of children as well as making sure that food and drinks are kept separate from any potential stray shards.

Another point worth considering is that you will be sitting for long periods of time, so it is wise to have a supportive chair and to make sure that your lower arms have space in front of you to rest on the table to avoid straining your wrists or shoulders.

## 1. ESSENTIAL TOOLS

Now let's look at the essential tools that you will need to start making mosaics.

A list of mosaic suppliers is included at the back of this book so please refer to the list to discover where to find the tools.

The tools you will need to make mosaics depend on the type of materials you are intending to use. Although I consider the six tools shown below to be essential for anyone interested in making mosaics, it is unlikely you will need all of them when you are getting started. Different tools are appropriate for different materials. To keep things simple at the beginning, I suggest that you invest in a pair of side biter nippers or compound nippers to work with unglazed ceramic, or the wheeled Leponitt cutters to use with glass.

The essential mosaic tool kit includes from left to right: a utility or Stanley knife with a sharp blade; Leponitt wheeled nippers; side biter tile nippers; compound nippers; angled tweezers and a mosaic pick set.

The side biter tile nippers and compound tile nippers do the same job, but the latter are a more expensive and rugged version of the simple side biters, which means they

**Basic mosaic tool kit.**

require less effort to cut. The compound tile nippers are highly recommended if you get the mosaic 'bug' and want a strong tool guaranteed to make easy work out of difficult cuts.

You will also need an adhesive spreader otherwise known as a dual head or double-sided spatula. The spreaders come in different sizes and are invaluable and versatile tools especially if you are planning to make mosaics with tile adhesive (see Chapters 13–15).

Further down the road you might get tempted by a hammer and hardie. This traditional mosaicist's tool has been used since the times of the Romans. As well as being used to cut marble and other types of stone it is ideal for cutting smalti, a specialist type of mosaic glass.

The hardie is a chisel-like blade set upside down into a wooden block. The blade may

**Dual head or double-sided spatula.**

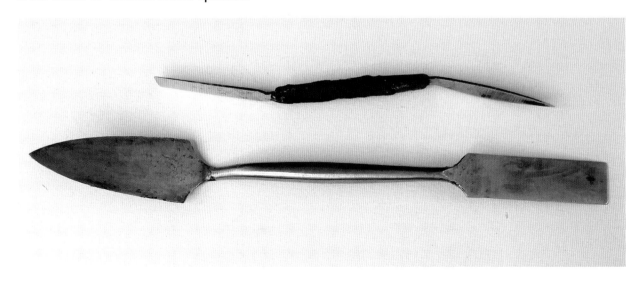

also come welded on to a metal base as in the photo. The material to be cut is then held in place over the blade and the weight of the hammer falling on to it will split it where required.

The hammers come in different weights, and will either be steel tipped (to cut stone) or carbide tipped (for smalti). There are also combination hammers which have a steel tip on one side and carbide on the other.

The hammer and hardie is for the serious mosaicist and although pricey, it is well worth the outlay and will last a lifetime.

**Hammer and hardie.**

## 2. EXTRA TOOLS

The more you make mosaics, the more you will want to equip yourself with extra tools to handle specific jobs. An electric screwdriver is helpful when you want to make holes in wood for hanging fittings and a jigsaw will allow you to cut substrates into precisely the shape that you want.

Another great tool is a flat bed tile cutter, the type used by tilers to cut kitchen and bathroom tiles. Although it looks like a serious bit of kit, it is relatively inexpensive and makes short work of cutting tiles.

**Jigsaw and electric drill.**

**Flat bed tile cutter.**

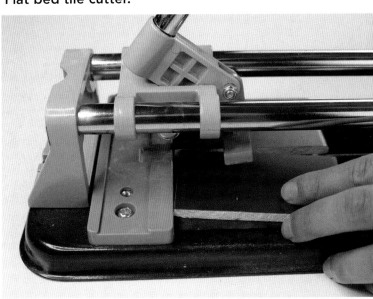

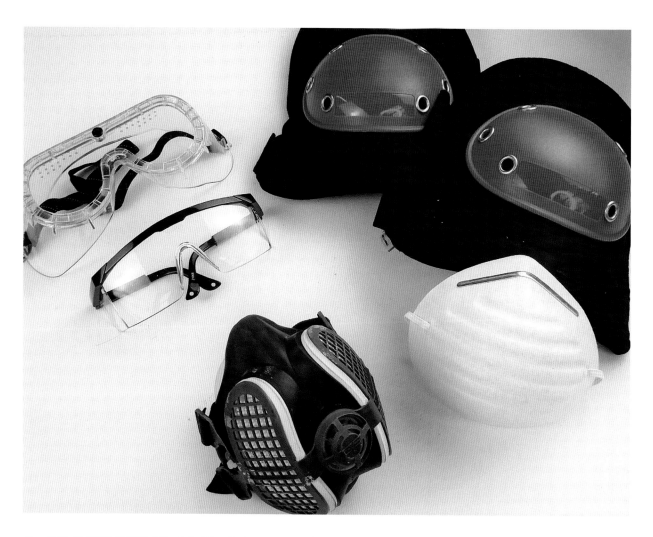

## 3. PROTECTIVE AND SAFETY EQUIPMENT

Accidents are extremely rare when making mosaics, but it is worth bearing in mind the potential risk of sharp shards particularly when you are cutting mosaic materials.

It is highly recommended that you invest in a pair of safety glasses or goggles which can be found at any hardware outlet, and you will also need a dust mask for mixing grout and tile adhesive. You can use lightweight, single-use dust masks, but it is worth buying a more efficient mask which has an effective filter and adjustable straps. Do not be tempted to cut corners on mask wearing – grout and tile adhesives are cement-based compounds which release fine dust when stirred which will cause damage to your lungs over a period of time.

Ordinary rubber kitchen gloves will also be needed for the messier aspects of mosaic making and you may also want to use disposable gloves when you are working with tile adhesive (also known as thinset mortar). If you are likely to be installing large-scale floor mosaics, then knee pads will make things easier.

## 4. DESIGN MATERIALS

Whichever kind of mosaics you are interested in making – from copies of ancient patterns to contemporary abstracts – you will need to plan your design before you start. Invest in a good set of coloured pencils, marker pens, a metal ruler and set square, carbon paper and plenty of plain paper to draw out your designs.

Design materials.

# 5. SUBSTRATES

From left to right: marine plywood, home-made substrate made of fibreglass mesh and tile adhesive/thinset mortar (see overleaf), Wedi board, fibreglass mesh, Jackoboard and a terracotta saucer.

Mosaics can be applied to a variety of different surfaces, from terracotta pots to wooden plaques, slate, hardie backer and home-made substrates. Substrates may also come in the form of pre-cut MDF shapes which make wonderful mosaic bases for indoor use.

The main thing to bear in mind is that some substrates will be better suited to outdoor installation than

Mosaic substrates.

*Home-made mesh and tile adhesive substrates provide versatile surfaces suitable for indoors and outdoors.*

**Materials for making your own mesh and tile adhesive substrates.**

## Materials:

• A plastic ground sheet – a builder's tarpaulin is ideal, but an ordinary shopping bag cut open so it lies flat will do the job just as well.

• Dry tile adhesive. I always buy the flexible adhesive that is suitable for outdoors. It comes as a white or grey powder and is usually sold in 20kg bags from tile suppliers. To make life easier it is a good idea to transfer some into a smaller lidded container which you can keep on your work table. However, BAL makes a tile adhesive called Mosaic Fix which comes in handy 1kg and 5kg bags.

• Dust mask

• An old yoghurt pot or similar container to mix the tile adhesive

• A spoon

• A water mister (if required)

• Fibreglass mesh cut into two similar sized pieces. The pieces can be any size or shape but the great thing about this substrate is that it is thin and lightweight so that you can shape it with ordinary kitchen scissors once it has dried.

• A spreading tool – an old supermarket loyalty or transport card will do the job.

## Method:

1. Lay the plastic covering over your work table and then mix the tile adhesive with water in a small container. Don't forget to wear your dust mask when you do this. Add the water slowly to make a paste-like mixture. It should not be too runny or too stiff. If you scoop some into the spoon and let it drop back into the bowl it should take a few seconds to fall. The amount of adhesive you will need will depend on the size of the substrate you are making.

Spread the tile adhesive thinly using the spreading tool.

2. Put one piece of the mesh on to the plastic and spread the tile adhesive thinly and evenly over it with the spreading tool. The adhesive will push through the mesh on to the plastic – this is fine. Lay the second piece of mesh over the first and repeat the process.

3. Leave the substrate to fully dry and then it will peel easily away from the plastic.

4. If you want an undulating surface, then pick up the two layers of mesh and fresh adhesive and lay them over a mould so that the substrate will shape itself around the mould.

others and some substrates need to be sealed or prepared before use to ensure that your mosaic will last a long time.

Marine plywood and MDF are both great indoor mosaic surfaces. Prepare the wood by first sanding it with rough sandpaper and scoring with a criss-cross pattern using a Stanley knife. Then combine PVA glue and water in a 50:50 ratio, mix well, brush on with a domestic brush and leave to dry.

Wedi board and Jackoboard are types of lightweight, compressed foam board which make ideal substrates for mosaics. The board is normally used in bathroom construction and so is suitable for wet conditions and it is also a practical option for outdoor installation. The board, which is found at tile suppliers, comes in various thicknesses and dimensions and can be easily cut down to the required size using a metal ruler and a utility knife with a sharp blade. Simply score the surface of the board several times against the edge of the ruler with the utility knife until the knife penetrates the thin surface layer of cement. Then the board will snap along the score line and the knife will easily cut through the rest of the board.

**Pre-cut MDF shapes.**

## 6. MOSAIC GLUES AND ADHESIVES

The main four glues that are needed for almost all mosaic projects are:

**General purpose PVA** which is great for all indoor projects where you are using flat, purpose-made mosaic tiles such as unglazed ceramic and vitreous glass.

**Titebond II Premium Wood Glue or Weldbond.** These indoor and outdoor glues are water resistant and perfect for all direct method mosaic projects. They do the same job as PVA but will never let you down.

**Tile adhesive.** Sold as a powder or in pre-mixed tubs. Simply add water to the powder to make a paste. As a rule, the powered version is suitable for outdoors whereas the premixed one can only be used for indoor projects. However, always check the contents description on the product. Both types of tile adhesive set hard after a few hours. I use BAL Max Flex Fibre,

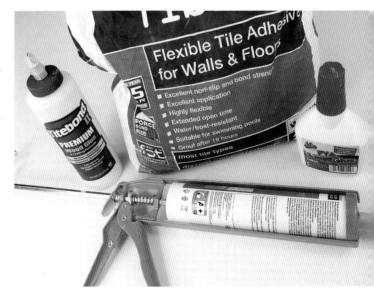
**Mosaic glues and adhesives.**

Flexible Tile Adhesive for Walls and Floors in white, which comes in 20kg bags.

**Silicone glue.** Sold in tubes in hardware shops which can be dispensed with a silicone 'gun' through a nozzle. If necessary, decant the silicone into small syringes so you have more control over the amount of glue dispensed.

### GROUT

Be sure to buy the appropriate grout for the job you are doing. In other words, is your mosaic going to be going indoors or outdoors? How wide are the gaps between your tesserae? Always check the manufacturer's description on the bag before you buy to be certain that it will be suitable for your job. I almost invariably use BAL Micromax II Wall and Flour Grout for joints from 1mm to 20mm in Smoke. For more on grouting see Chapter 9.

## 7. FINISHING AND HANGING

Your approach to finishing and hanging your mosaic will depend on the size and type of substrate you are using and where the mosaic will be hung.

### WOOD

For mosaics on wood, a simple approach is to paint the sides and back before you begin work. For smaller work you would then screw one or two D-ring picture hangers on to the back on completion. For larger pieces that are going to be set into a permanent location, it is best to drill countersunk holes before you begin work. The mosaic will then be screwed into the wall and the holes covered with tesserae and grouted at the end. The pre-painted edges can be left as they are or edged with copper foil tape.

Alternatively, to hang the mosaic you can use French cleats which are two lengths of wood approximately 8cm thick which are cut slightly shorter than the length of the mosaic. The wood is cut in half using a saw set at a 45-degree angle. One piece is fastened to the wall with its slanting edge facing up. The other piece is attached to the back of the item you're hanging on the wall, with its slanting edge facing down so that they slot into each other.

A frame is also an option. If so, it is advisable to frame the mosaic before you start work. Ideally, the frame would be a shallow tray made at the same height as the tesserae so that the finished work is flush with the frame. Paint the frame before you begin mosaicking. It will need touching up after grouting but painting first is much easier than trying to avoid getting paint on your completed mosaic.

### WEDI OR JACKOBOARD

If needed, protect the edges of the foam board with fibreglass mesh tape before mosaicking. The tape, which is otherwise called scrim or plasterboard tape, is sticky and easily folds over the sides of the board, giving them extra strength. When the work is being grouted, run a finger of grout along the sides to create a thin layer which will cover the tape and seal the exposed foam. The grout can be painted once it has dried.

Wedi and Jackoboard are relatively soft and will not sustain the weight of a large or heavy mosaic. In this case, it is best to have a tray frame made in advance with holes left in the back struts so that the mosaic can be screwed into place in the same way as described opposite except without the D-rings.

For smaller mosaics on foam board, apply the hanging fittings before you start mosaicking. You will either need one or two each of the tee nuts, screws, etc. depending on the size of the mosaic.

## Materials
• Wedi or Jackoboard, 120mm–150mm thick
• 1 x 4mm tee nuts
• 1 x 4mm cheese head screws, the length will depend on how thick your board is
• 1 x 4mm picture hanging D-rings
• 1 x 6mm washers
• Thin sharp instrument such as a mosaic pick

## Method
1. Mark where the hole is going to be on your board.

2. Use a thin sharp instrument to create a hole.

3. Press a tee nut over the hole into the foam board.

4. Turn the foam board over.

5. Put the screw through the D-ring and then through the washer.

6. Position the washer over the hole (on the reverse side from the tee nut) and turn the screw so that it catches with the tee nut.

7. Tighten it but be careful – you want the tee nut to be flush with the surface of the foam board so that you can mosaic over it, but if you tighten it too much the foam board will collapse. Do it slowly.

Use a thin sharp instrument to create a hole.

Turn the screw so that it catches with the tee nut.

# CHAPTER 3:
# MOSAIC MATERIALS

CHOOSING YOUR MATERIALS is probably the most important part of the process of designing and making a mosaic. Whether you decide to use muted ceramic, vibrant glass, your granny's broken wedding china or pebbles carefully collected over years of country walks, that choice will influence how you approach the work as well as the overall effect and feel of the finished mosaic.

When it comes to mosaic materials, there is almost no limit to what you can use. Mosaic suppliers stock a range of purpose-made flat glass and ceramic tiles of different sizes alongside smalti (a richly coloured specialist glass made in Italy), mirrored tiles, glass nuggets and shapes, and other materials such as millefiori.

However, you do not have to open your wallet to start making mosaics. Pebbles, broken crockery, sea glass and old costume jewellery are great options, and you can also explore using single-use plastics, ring pulls, bottle tops, defunct wires and electronics, discarded toys and anything else that is water resistant and reasonably easy to cut or break. Canadian artist Julie Sperling is one of many mosaicists who use leftover coloured tile adhesive (thinset mortar) to create tesserae which are incorporated into her pieces.

**Enough (Talk). Tesserae made of leftover tile adhesive. Julie Sperling.**

Blue Bird with Leaves. Unglazed ceramic and vitreous glass. Helen Miles.

## SHOP BOUGHT

**Unglazed ceramic tiles and vitreous glass tiles.** Unglazed ceramic tiles come in a range of muted earthy colours which make great stand-ins for natural stone. Vitreous glass tiles are available in a much wider range of colours, including bright tones. Both of these purpose-made tiles have a ridged side and a smooth side. The ridged side is designed to be placed downwards aiding adhesion, but many mosaic artists like to use the textured ridges as part of their artistic designs. The tiles are sold glued on to full, half or quarter sheets of paper which need to be soaked in water, so the glue dissolves and the tiles easily peel away.

The great advantage of the unglazed ceramic and many of the glass tiles is that they are a standard thickness of 4mm and are suitable for outdoor work, meaning they can used together in the same mosaic without losing the flat surface. These tiles can also be applied easily with glue, and they are an obvious choice for mosaics which are made using the direct method and are grouted once the work is complete.

**Other types of glass tiles** are also widely used in mosaic art, including iridescent, gold-veined and transparent glass, as well as stained glass, mirror, glass gems and even crash glass. Each has its own properties and can be mixed with other materials. However, because of the different thicknesses, they are either used separately or applied using tile adhesive (thinset mortar) (see Chapters 13–15) to create a deliberately textured surface.

**Millefiori** is a particular type of glass traditionally produced in Murano, Italy, although there is now a fused glass version made in China. Literally meaning 'a thousand flowers', millefiori are circular glass pieces of various sizes which often come with embedded flower designs or concentric circles. Millefiori 'eyes' are a wonderful option for animals' faces, and they add a burst of colour to any mosaic but some are thicker than others, so they are not suitable if a flat surface is required.

**Pink Pheasant. Millefiori and vitreous glass. Martin Cheek.**

**Glazed ceramic tiles.** The size and thickness of these tiles vary, but a popular option is Cinca glazed tiles, which are manufactured in Portugal. Cinca are architectural tiles, suitable for indoors and outdoors, including floors, and they are highly durable and frost proof. If your mosaic is for indoors then you can use ordinary kitchen or bathroom tiles. Both Cinca or indoor domestic tiles can be cut with side biters or a flat bed tile cutter. Ragged edges can be smoothed down with a ceramic tile file – available at most tile suppliers or large hardware shops.

Detail of The Treatment Rooms, decorated by Carrie Reichardt and volunteers using outdoor-grade glazed ceramic tiles. Chiswick, London, UK.

**Stained glass.** There are many mosaic artists who specialise in using stained glass in their work. The advantage of the glass is that it comes in large sheets which can be cut down to any size and shape using a glass scorer. Stained glass

**Mutation. Inspired by Van Gogh's irises, this work is made with stained glass on tempered glass. John Sollinger.**

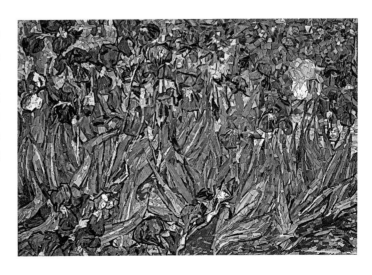

elements can be incorporated into a mosaic which includes other materials. Stained glass can also be bought in pre-cut squares.

**Smalti.** Smalti is a handmade compressed glass, which is traditionally made in Italy although alternatives are now produced in Mexico and China. The glass comes in an enormous range of subtle and striking colours and is usually bought in pre-cut miniature 'bricks' which are sold in bags from 50g upwards as single colours or in coordinated mixtures. Smalti can also be bought in 'pizzas', large discs of glass which can be bought whole or in quarters. Smalti has been prized since Byzantine times for its reflective qualities and is still widely used by contemporary artists. Gold leaf smalti is made by mounting a layer of gold over glass and then sealing it with another thin layer of transparent glass so that the gold seems to be on the surface. Occasional air bubbles produced during the heating process means that smalti may have little holes, so grouting is best avoided. Smalti can be cut with a hammer and hardie or with wheeled glass nippers.

**Detail from a mosaic mural. Glasgow Central station, Scotland, UK. Smalti, including a sun made out of a whole smalti 'pizza'. Jude Burkhauser.**

Insert for a closed off fireplace. Greek marble made on mesh (see Chapter 10). Helen Miles.

The Lion and the Snake. Pebbles. Maggy Howarth.

**Marble and stone.** If you are lucky enough to live in a part of the world where marble occurs naturally, then of course you can collect it yourself and break the marble down into tesserae with your hammer and hardie. Alternatively, polished marble tiles can be bought at regular tile suppliers. Some mosaic suppliers also sell unpolished marble in metre length rods. Marble and stone can be bought in a range of soft, muted earthy colours. It is a porous material so needs to be sealed, and unpolished marble often has a slightly pitted surface making it unsuitable for grouting.

**Pebbles.** Pebbles that are suitable for making mosaics can be bought from specialist suppliers and garden centres but bear in mind that it is illegal in the UK to remove pebbles from the beach.

Mosaics made with pebbles require considerable labour and skill to produce. The method invented by UK-based pebble mosaic expert Maggy Howarth involves carefully sorting the stones and packing them tightly into a mould following a pattern which has been reversed. A centimetre of sand is brushed around each pebble to keep it upright. A grout slurry is then poured over them, followed by concrete. Once the concrete has set, the mould is turned over and removed and the sand brushed off to reveal the mosaic.

## FOUND AND RECYCLED

**China and pottery.** There cannot be a kitchen in the country or perhaps in the world which does not produce a steady supply of broken china and pottery. Pieces which have been part of a family for decades are often kept long after their handles have fallen off or deep cracks have ended their years of faithful service. Mosaics made of china and pottery constitute a sub-branch of the mosaic world, known as pique assiette mosaics, a French term associated with Raymond Isidore's famous Maison Pique Assiette in Chartres,

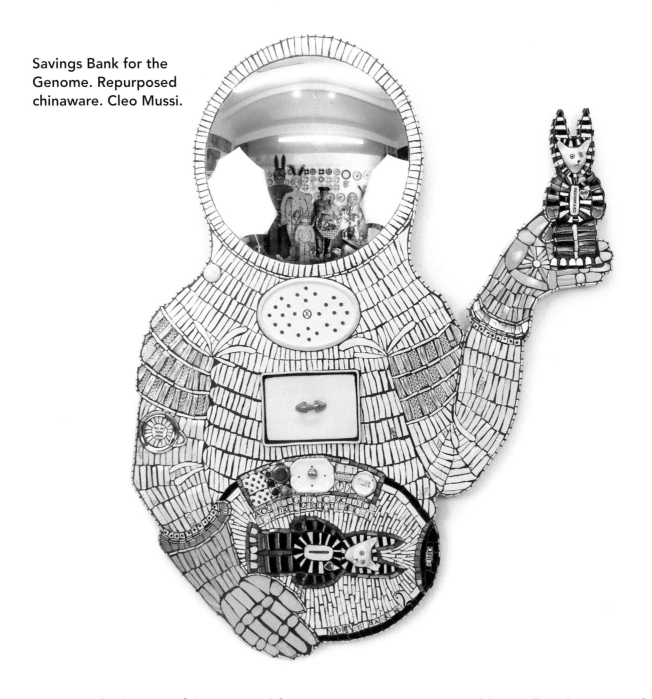

Savings Bank for the Genome. Repurposed chinaware. Cleo Mussi.

France. The beauty of this material for mosaics is that it is accessible to all and is a way of repurposing treasured items. China and pottery can be cut easily with ordinary side biter or wheeled nippers. If you want a more precise cut, then use a Dremel rotary tool.

**Beach-foraged materials:** The beach is an ideal place to find materials to use for mosaics. Sea glass, wave-worn brick, shells, and pottery fragments are among the items that can be collected on the shore and the process of looking for beach 'treasure' can be a rewarding part of the mosaic-making process. Do not remove shells which have living organisms inside them, and anything found on the beach must be thoroughly washed and rinsed to clean away any salt residue. Sea estuaries near ports are particularly fruitful places to search for pottery fragments, as ships once used broken crockery as ballast – which was discarded when it was no longer needed.

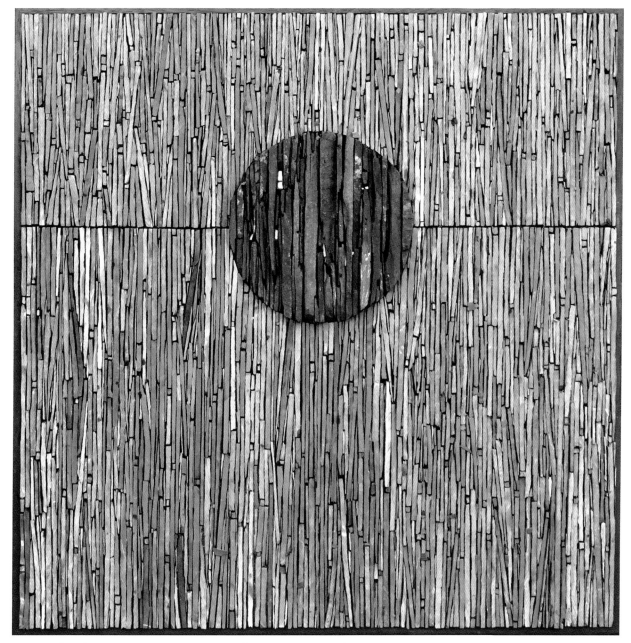

Xenolith. Slate and Italian gold leaf smalti. Dugald MacInnes.

**Slate.** Slate is a wonderfully versatile material to use in mosaic making and comes in different shades of light and dark grey, often with green or purple tinges. The beauty of working with slate is that it can have lighter veins or little nuggets of pyrite crystal, adding interest to the piece. Broken slate can be found in the vicinity of disused slate mines and suppliers of roof tiles will be happy to allow you to help yourself to their discarded stock. Larger pieces of slate need to be cut with a wet saw, but smaller pieces can be broken down with a hammer and hardie, hammer and chisel or simple side biters.

**Single-use plastics and general household rubbish:** Plastic cutlery, bottle tops, straws, aluminium cans, tubes and containers, disused toys and game parts, and old electronics if they cannot be safely recycled in other ways are just some items that can be incorporated into mosaics. Artists who use rubbish include Francesca Busca who makes mosaics out of

**Connections, detail. 100 per cent rubbish: 10 years' worth of unwanted cables. Francesca Busca.**

100 per cent waste, including plastic fruit nets, drinks cans, paper, lids, cables and even tea bags.

**Miscellaneous:** Beads, broken jewellery, hardware, coins, inside of clocks and watches, buttons – as long as the materials have a flat side which can be reasonably easily cut if needed then almost anything goes.

# CHAPTER 4:

# CUTTING AND GLUING TECHNIQUES

ALWAYS WEAR SAFETY goggles to protect your eyes before you start cutting mosaic materials. Accidents from making mosaics are rare, but it is advisable to take sensible precautions. Having a dustpan and brush handy is also a good idea, as cutting mosaic tiles creates a lot of dust and shards.

Do not be surprised if the tile does not cut the way you expect or want it to. Winckelmans unglazed ceramic tiles can split in unpredictable ways, some colours can be easier than others, and you may find that different batches of the same colour will respond differently to the tool – it's to do with the batch firing not your mosaic skills.

The key thing to remember is that the beauty of mosaic lies in the handmade feel of the work. Perfectly cut tiles would not have the same effect. Also, even the wobbliest of cuts will find a good home so put them on one side and have another go.

## CUTTING WINCKELMANS UNGLAZED CERAMIC WITH SIDE BITER NIPPERS

1. Hold the nippers in one hand with your grip towards the end of the handles. If you look at the tool from above, you will see the head of the nippers has a curved side and a flat side. Holding the nippers as an extension of your forearm, make sure that the curved side of the nippers is facing towards your empty hand.

2. To cut the tile in half, creating two rectangles, hold it between the thumb and two forefingers. Place the edge of the tool halfway down the tile. Make sure that you only put the tile two or three millimetres under the blades of the tool. The further you put the tile under the blades, the harder it will be to cut, so only place it right on the edge of the tool. Apply gentle pressure to the handles of the tool and the tile will snap in two.

3. To cut a circle, it sometimes helps to use a pencil to draw on the tile where you want the

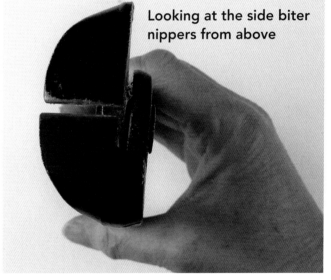

Looking at the side biter nippers from above

Place the tile on the edge of the blades.

Cutting a circle.

cuts to be. In this case, place the blades fully across the line of the cut you wish to create and press down firmly on the handles.

4. Cutting unglazed ceramic tiles with compound nippers requires the same process. The only difference is that the tool head does not have a curved side and flat side, so it does not matter which way the head is facing. As with the side biter nippers, make sure your hand is towards the end of the handles rather than close to the head.

## CUTTING VITREOUS GLASS WITH WHEELED NIPPERS

1. Hold the wheeled nippers with the blade side of the tool head facing towards your other hand.

2. Place the wheeled blades *fully over* the line of the cut that you wish to create. Unlike with the unglazed ceramic you do not place the blades on the edge of the tile.

3. Squeeze the handles of the tool gently together. The glass will cut easily with very little pressure and will feel like butter compared to the unglazed ceramic.

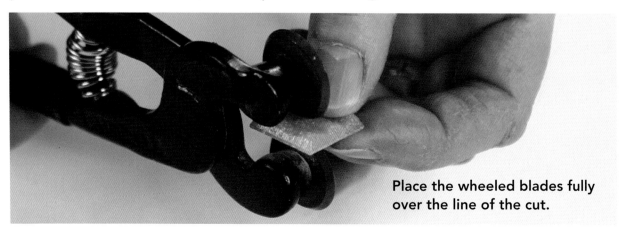

**Place the wheeled blades fully over the line of the cut.**

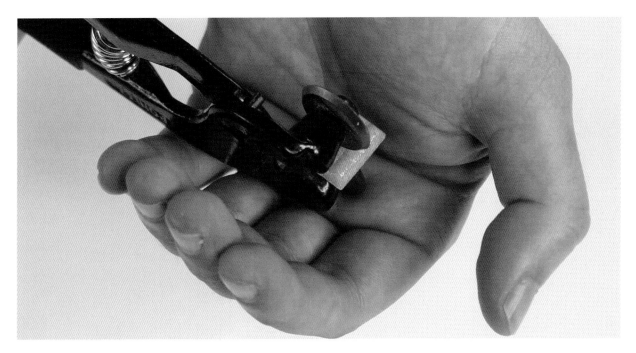

**Cup your hand around the tile.**

4. Another way to prevent shards escaping is to cup your hand around the tile as you cut or to cut into a box placed on its side in front of you.

## CUTTING SMALTI OR STONE WITH THE HAMMER AND HARDIE

Hammers sold as companion tools to the hardie come in different weights, starting at 450g. Which one you choose depends on your personal preference. Be sure to have the right hammer for the right material – carbide tipped for smalti, or steel for stone. You can buy combination hammers with carbide on one side and steel on the other.

1. Hold the hammer about a finger's length from the head. With your arm bent at the elbow, think of the hammer as an extension of your forearm.

2. Place the material over the blade of the hardie, holding it firmly between your finger and thumb.

3. The blade of the hammer should be directly above the hardie as it falls and strikes the material.

**Avoid the hammer striking the hardie after the cut.**

4. It is the weight of the hammer rather than the force of the body that causes the material to split so only your hand and wrist will move rather than the forearm. Be careful to avoid the hammer striking the hardie after the cut, as it will quickly blunt the blade.

## GLUING TECHNIQUE

The following technique is used with either PVA, Weldbond, or Titebond II glues for the direct mosaic method (see Chapter 5). The technique for tile adhesive/thinset mortar is covered in Chapters 13–15.

It is important to avoid getting glue on the front of the tiles. Even though the glue is transparent, when it dries it will show up after grouting as milky blotches which will be impossible to remove, so keep a piece of kitchen roll nearby and wipe off any excess glue quickly.

1. Squeeze a dollop of glue into a clean shallow lid. I never use glue directly from the bottle as having a small quantity gives you greater control and ensures that you work neatly. Pick up each individual tessera and dip it lightly into the glue.

2. Place the tessera on to the substrate. Press it down with one finger to ensure contact between the board and the tile, and then do not disturb it unless necessary.

3. If you find it difficult to avoid getting glue on your hands, then hold the tessera with angled tweezers.

**Hold the tessera with angled tweezers.**

4. Alternatively, you can use a glue brush to apply a small amount of glue on to the mosaic substrate. Apply just enough to glue three or four tesserae. Avoid putting too much glue on to the surface because dried glue will prevent subsequent pieces from sitting flat. Remove excess glue with a mosaic pick before it dries.

5. To retain more control over the application of the glue, you can dip the back of a plastic spoon lightly into the glue and then dab the individual tesserae on to the glue on the spoon. This technique cuts down the possibility of mess and means that you are using only small quantities of glue at a time – you simply 'refill' the spoon as needed. The advantage of using a plastic spoon is that the old glue will easily peel off once it is dry so you can reuse the same spoon multiple times.

**Remove excess glue with a mosaic pick.**

CHAPTER 5:

# LEARNING FROM THE ANCIENTS — PLANNING

CREATING A SUCCESSFUL mosaic design relies on the essential principles of all good composition. Think about the rule of thirds, the negative space (the non-focal part of the design) and creating balance in your piece. One of the best ways to learn about artistic design is to spend time in art galleries and look at professional photographs – even advertisements in magazines. You will soon see that the principles are applied across a range of media.

As for the art of mosaics, visit historic mosaic sites, look at mosaics in public spaces and online and follow contemporary mosaic artists on social media. By looking at mosaics in this way you will be opening the door on to a rich tradition which encompasses a dizzying range of artistry, technique and geographical location.

You will quickly discover that there are many ways to make mosaics and that no single way is more correct or authentic than any other. However, whether you are looking for helpful ground rules as you start your mosaic journey or a way of developing your practice

**Cricket detail in a border, The Judgement of Paris, Louvre, Paris. Second century CE.**

as you get deeper into the art, I think it is useful to begin by looking at the classical 'rules' of mosaics.

These rules cover the fundamental principles of how to think about designing a mosaic as well as cutting, laying and spacing your tesserae (covered in Chapter 6). They have been used since the times of the ancient Romans and continue to be employed by twenty-first-century mosaicists. In many ways, therefore, they are the bedrock of mosaic practice in all its many forms.

The more time you spend with ancient mosaics the more you will notice the sophistication of Roman designs. Intricate patterns, careful shading, unexpected details, and stark story telling are all part of the wonder of ancient mosaics. It is important to stress, however, that although we can learn from the ancients, we are not seeking to copy them.

The crucial difference between floors which once adorned baptistries and palaces, and contemporary mosaic art is the scale and the manner in which Roman floors were made. In many cases these 'carpets' of stone covered extensive areas and were usually made by a team of workers pressing individual tesserae into wet mortar on site. Mosaics are rarely made in this way nowadays and although there have been occasional replicas of ancient mosaics, it would be pointless to try and recreate a Roman design piece by piece. Mosaics created in the studio by an individual artist tend to have greater attention paid to the placement of the individual tesserae than work made by their ancient counterparts.

**Hunting dog, detail. Heraclea Lyncestis, Northern Macedonia. Sixth century CE.**

**Mosaic artist Joanna Kessel at work in her Edinburgh studio.** Photo: David Kessel

## DESIGN FUNDAMENTALS

The first thing to bear in mind when designing a mosaic is to remember the obvious: mosaics are made of numerous bits. That means that they are visually busy; there is a lot going on even before you think about the design, whether it be an abstract piece or a figurative one. When you look at Roman mosaics you will see that the designs usually have a pared-down simplicity to them even though they can be quite complex. By simplicity I mean that they have clear outlines and areas of focus which means that the image is easy to 'read'. The bold, clean lines of linocut prints are similar.

A basic principle of mosaic is that a great deal can be implied by the placing of relatively few tesserae. Look at the image of the hunting dog tied to a tree. The essential features of the animal – the eye, mouth, and teeth – are depicted with only a few pieces. Leaving aside the sub-genre of micro mosaics, it is best to avoid too much detail in your design for the simple reason that the greater the detail, the smaller the tesserae need to be.

### SPACE

This clarity is partly achieved by leaving space around the individual elements. The space is normally created with the background tone, which is usually (but not always) a lighter shade than the foreground. Leaving space around the main design/s alleviates

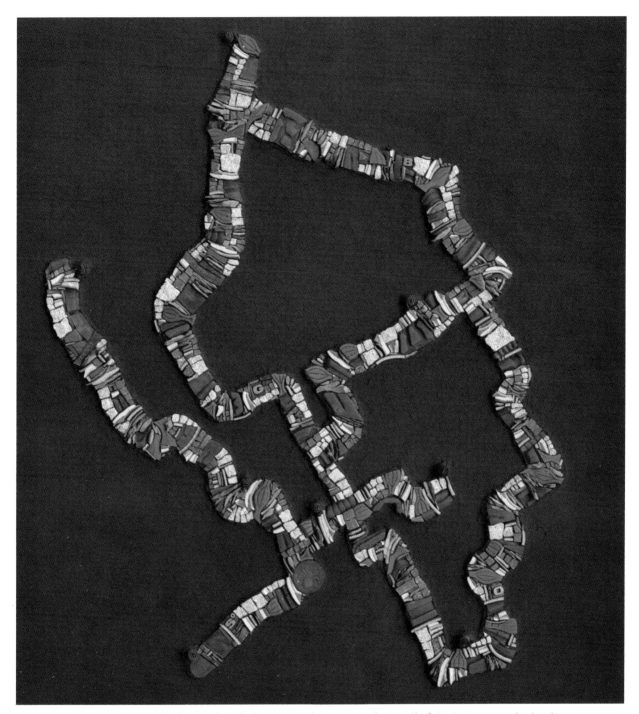

The Paths Most Travelled. Redback boot (right), Bogs boot (left). Cement, shale, limestone. Julie Sperling.

the visual overstimulation which can occur if there is too much happening in a single mosaic. Contemporary mosaicists often recreate this sense of space by leaving parts of the mosaic substrate untessellated.

## CONTRAST

Ancient mosaics rely heavily on contrast to achieve visual clarity. This is similar to the concept of space, but it also includes thinking about the tones and colours that you are planning to use. The ancients only had stone (or occasionally faience and ceramic) to work

**The Weight of Words. Slate and smalti. Rachel Davies.**

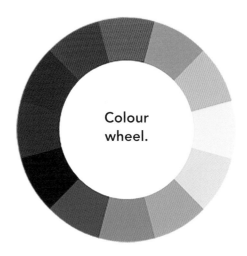

Colour wheel.

with, so their designs tend to rely on contrasting tones to make the main design elements stand out. Today's mosaic artists have an enormous range of materials to choose from and it is tempting to get swept up in the beauty and variety of the options. But less is more when it comes to mosaics. Squint your eyes or take a photo on your phone and convert it to grayscale to get a sense of the contrasts inherent in the materials.

Pay particular attention to colour. Using a colour wheel can be helpful when you are thinking about putting colours together in a mosaic. Colours which are opposite each other on the wheel are 'complementary' which means that they provide a good way of creating contrast. Ones which are next to each the other on the wheel are 'harmonious' which means they blend together.

Some of the best designs are achieved by simple contrasts: light/dark (like the ancients), or bright/dull, textured/smooth, shiny/matt, tight/open (placing of the tesserae), large/small (size of tesserae) and so on.

### BORDERS

It is often difficult to decide whether to create a border around your mosaic design. It might be a plain frame of a different coloured tile or a more elaborate repetitive border. Almost all ancient mosaics have borders which are as thoughtfully considered and intricate

**Think about your border early in the design process. Homecoming Birds. Marble. Helen Miles.**

as the main design. This is a lesson for contemporary makers. Do not leave the planning of the border (if any) until the end but think about it as part of your early design process. A border can hold and contain the design, but it can also distract from it or even squeeze it, making the mosaic feel crowded.

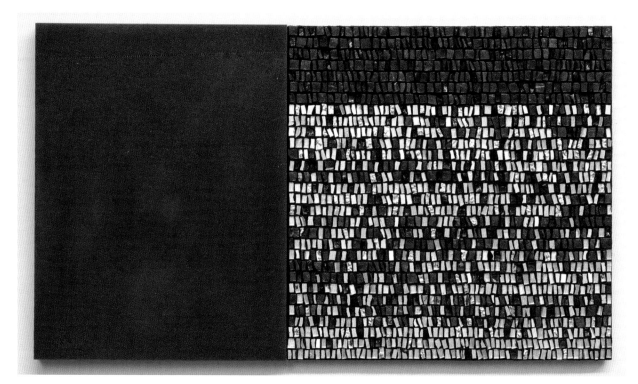

(In)visible Cities Interface IV. Smalti, 24K gold leaf mosaic, marble and Jesomite. **Joanna Kessel.** Photo: Michael Wolchover

## PATTERN

Pattern in Roman mosaics is too large a subject to cover here, but suffice to say that pattern is a crucial, uniting factor in many ancient designs. The reliance on pattern in ancient mosaics to hold the design together and keep it visually interesting is instructive. Many mosaic artists use pattern, in other words repeated elements, as the core of their work. Once again, it does not need to be complicated. Mosaic materials themselves can often be the 'subject' of a piece and laying them in repeat patterns can be extremely effective.

## CONTEXT

Finally, the ancients planned their mosaics carefully according to the context in which they would be seen. The mosaic might be the first thing you would encounter as you entered a private space, like the famous Beware of the Dog designs in Pompeii, or be part of a display of wealth and largesse laid out in the public rooms for guests to admire, like the ubiquitous 'hospitality' mosaics in ancient reception rooms.

This attention to context is an important consideration when planning a mosaic. As mentioned above, a mosaic is visually stimulating so the room/wall/outdoor space in which it is going to be placed needs to be considered. Ideally, there will be nothing around it that competes or clashes.

Think about how the mosaic will be viewed. If it's going to

**East Meets West. Concrete tesserae and smalti. Anabella Wewer.** Photo: Bri Santoro

be a splashback behind a sink, then people washing their hands are going to have time to look at it closely. But if it's going into an arch above a doorway, then it's less likely that people will spend time contemplating it but will enjoy the burst of colour or elegant lines of the design.

The Ruins Project in Pennsylvania, USA, is a large-scale outdoor mosaic installation in the ruins of a former coal mine. Mosaic artists from all over the world have contributed site-specific work which has been designed and made for the setting, including this work by American artist Anabella Wewer, which is about the connection between the coal and the steel industries.

## COLOUR BLENDING

Look closely ... s and you will see that different areas of colour are blended
... a band or section of one colour followed by another, you
... olour gradually merge into each other. This bird illustrates
... rk outline on the duck's breast. Moving inwards, the dark
... red tones which in turn are interspersed with ochre which
... eces. This principle is consistently used in contemporary
... nse of colours amalgamating.

... um of Thessaloniki, Greece. Sixth century CE.

# CHAPTER 6:

# LEARNING FROM THE ANCIENTS – PRINCIPLES

THESE ARE THE key principles of mosaic making as practiced since ancient times.

## 1. NO GRIDS

When you are making mosaics, it is important to remember that the spaces between the tesserae are as much a part of the visual effect of the work as the tesserae themselves. The spaces, or interstices, can create lines within the mosaic which might be desirable as part of the design. However, if they are not part of the effect you want to create then there

**Grids create straight lines and crosses.**

are ways to avoid them being distracting to the eye. The first principle is to never lay your tesserae in a grid pattern. Grids create straight lines running between the tesserae both horizontally and vertically, as well as crosses which can lead to unwanted focal points.

The way to prevent this is to offset the tesserae like bricks in a wall but this still leaves horizontal straight lines.

Tilt every third or fourth tessera to break up the horizontal lines. Now there are no straight lines or crosses.

**Offset the tesserae.**

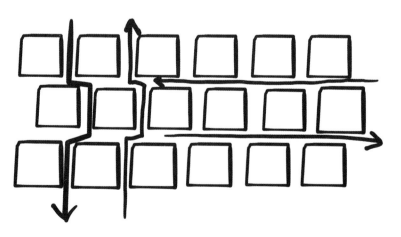

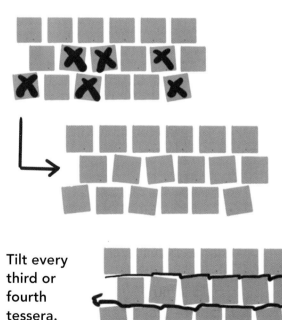

**Tilt every third or fourth tessera.**

**Pen & Sword Books** have over 4000 books currently available, our imprints include; Aviation, Naval, Military, Archaeology, Transport, Frontline, Seaforth and the Battleground series, and we cover all periods of history on land, sea and air.

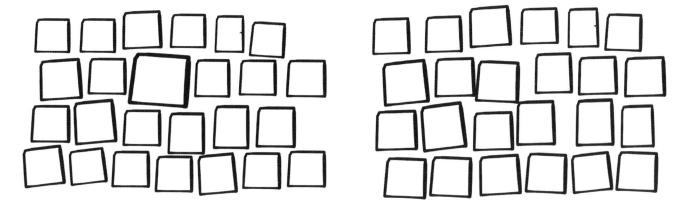

Inconsistency of size.

Inconsistency of spacing.

## 2. CONSISTENCY

Keep the sizes of the tesserae and the interstices between them reasonably consistent. If you introduce significant variations in the size of the tesserae or in the gaps between them, then this also creates unwanted focal points. Obviously, slight variations are fine and are part of the beauty of the work. This principle only applies to mosaic work where the artist has chosen to use the same tesserae throughout, most commonly squares. Contemporary mosaic artists often use variety in the size and shape of the tesserae for deliberate design purposes.

## 3. AVOID TRIANGLES UNLESS YOU NEED THEM

Triangles act like arrows in your piece, attracting the eye to a particular point. So only use triangles if they are needed or wanted. In this flower, for example, the triangle at the point of the petal emphasises the shape of the petal. However, internal triangles would be distracting. If you need a triangle-like shape, then nip off the tip to take away the arrow-like quality of the shape.

**Nip off the tips of superfluous triangles.**

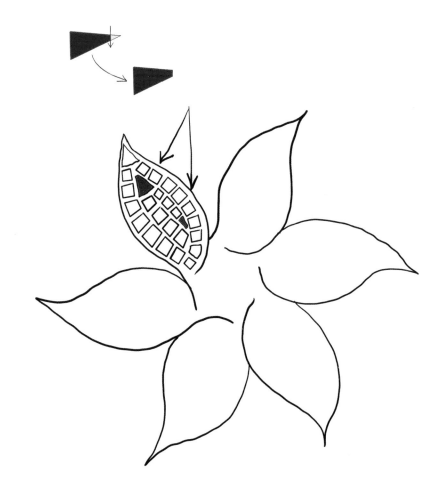

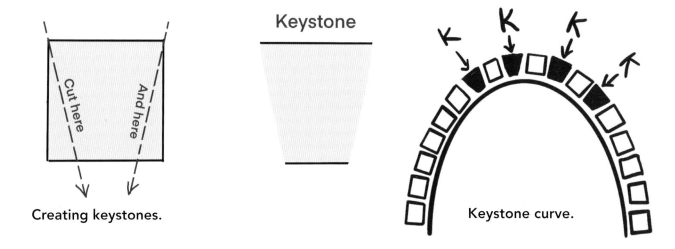

Keystone

Creating keystones.

Keystone curve.

## 4. USE KEYSTONES WHEN CREATING CURVES

This is a keystone. It is a square with the two parallel sides cut off at an angle. Keystones help you create smooth curves so that you don't have to use slivers or awkward shapes.

## 5. SDOPPIAMENTO: LINES SPLITTING AND MERGING AS THE SPACE EXPANDS OR CONTRACTS

This is the principle of splitting one line into two or merging two lines into one when needed to fill a space. This splitting and re-converging is done when a line needs to expand or contract – to fill a wider space or a narrower one. Let's take a bird's wing as an example. The space filled by Tessera A is the wing tip, but as the mosaic progresses towards the base of the wing, the space expands. Instead of using larger and larger tesserae in order to fill the space, the line splits, and then splits again as needed. The red tesserae mark where the split occurs. This splitting is a way to keep reasonable size consistency in the tesserae and is used in interesting and innovative ways by contemporary mosaicists.

**Lines splitting and merging.**

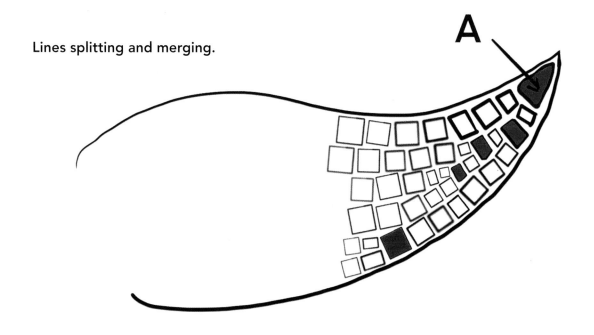

**Start with the main focus of the design.**          **Outline the design in the background colour.**

## 6. ORDER OF WORK

Start with the centre or the main focus of the design, in this case the centre of the flower, and then build up the rest of the design. Next lay a line of tesserae in the background colour, outlining the design. Finally lay the framing tesserae and fill in the background.

**Lay the framing tesserae (shown in blue) and fill in the background.**

## 7. PEPPERING IN THE BACKGROUND

The Romans used materials such as stone and marble in their work and the naturally occurring variations in the colours means that there are always subtle changes in the background tones. The Byzantines took this to a new level by melding and merging different colours into their backgrounds, making them a lively and interesting component of the work. The effect can be replicated easily by adding a number of different shades of the same colour into the background of your mosaic or introducing stronger colours which work well with the foreground. This is called peppering.

**'Unswept Floor' wedding mosaic. Winckelmans unglazed ceramic. Helen Miles.**

## 8. OPUS

As well as applying these principles in their work, ancient mosaicists established a number of standard ways to lay the background of a mosaic. Here are the most common:

• *Opus Tessalatum.* Laying the background tesserae in fairly straight, offset rows. It has a non-obtrusive effect so that the eye is drawn to the focal point of the design.

**Opus Tessalutum. Pigeon detail, Lod Mosaic. Third century CE.**

Opus Vermiculatum. Detail of a floor mosaic of fishes and marine life. House of the Faun, Naples Archaeological Museum, Italy. Second century CE.

• *Opus Vermiculatum.* The name refers to the 'worm-like' quality of the work. Vermiculatum is a fine, detailed laying technique using small tesserae which are closely set with the aim of producing painterly effects with gradations of colour. The technique was especially used in ancient emblemata – the central motifs of early floor designs.

• *Opus Paladanium.* Or what we would call crazy paving. It is deceptively difficult to do well on a small scale. However, it's a useful opus for large background spaces and is popular for community projects.

Opus Paladanium. Pepper detail, Green Star Movement Mosaics, Whole Foods, Chicago.

• *Opus Musivum:* Entails laying the lines of the background so that they radiate out from the design like ripples in a pond. This style of laying brings movement and liveliness to the mosaic. See Bardo Fish, Chapter 7.

• *Opus Regulatum.* The tesserae are laid in a grid. This is rarely used but sometimes occurs in large-scale work. When used, the other design elements seem to be laid on top as if they are floating.

Contemporary mosaic artists have expanded this range of options, for example by choosing to mix shapes in their backgrounds (e.g. using both squares and rectangles) or by using different styles of opus in a single work to define and delineate various sections of the mosaic.

Deciding how to lay your background is a crucial part of the planning process when designing a mosaic. The grout lines which are created throughout the work, particularly in the background, should enhance and reflect whatever it is that your mosaic is trying to say or depict. In this mosaic you can see that I have used the grout lines to make leaf shapes, shadowing the leaves in the main design.

**Branches and leaves. Winckelmans unglazed ceramic. Helen Miles.**

# CHAPTER 7:

# LEARNING FROM THE ANCIENTS – PRACTICE

## WINCKELMANS UNGLAZED CERAMIC ON MARINE PLYWOOD

Ancient mosaics are a wonderful, copyright free source of design ideas. For our first project I have taken this fish from a large fourth century CE floor mosaic originally from Carthage and now in the Bardo Museum, Tunisia. Fish and birds are common designs in mosaics, ancient and modern, and their natural patterning makes them ideal subjects for the medium.

The fish is made on a piece of 10mm thick marine plywood measuring 26cm wide by 61cm long. Remember that wood is not recommended for outdoors, especially in exposed or wet conditions, unless you apply a few coats of yacht varnish to all the non-

**Fish detail from floor mosaic of fish, molluscs and ducks. Bardo Museum, Tunisia. Fourth century CE.**

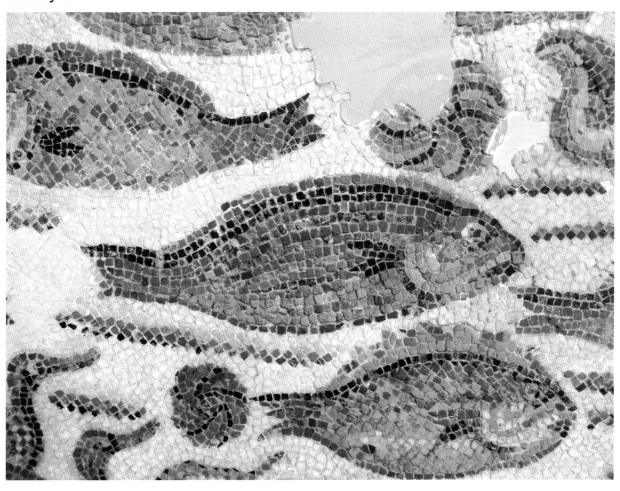

mosaicked parts. The varnish needs to be renewed every few years to protect the wood, so for outdoor work Wedi or Jackoboard is recommended (see Chapter 8).

First prepare the wood:

## Materials:
- Marine plywood board, 120–150mm thick
- Sandpaper (medium grade)
- Stanley or utility knife
- PVA glue
- Domestic paint brush (5cm or wider)
- Clean jam jar
- Wood primer and paint in a colour of your choice

## Method:
1. Use the sandpaper to rub the front of the board. Brush away the dust.

2. Get a Stanley knife and score the front of the board in a criss-cross pattern.

3. Prepare a 50:50 mixture of PVA glue and water in a jar. Mix well until the glue has dissolved into the water.

4. Apply the gluey water mixture to the front of the board with a paint brush and wait for it to dry (it won't take long).

5. Paint the back of the board with one coat of wood primer, allow to dry and then apply at least one coat of paint. Tip: paint the sides of your board first so that you can still pick the board up and turn it around as you paint the back.

**Paint the back and sides of the board.**

To make the fish you will need:

## Materials:
- Mosaic design
- Carbon paper
- Pencil
- Side biter nippers or compound nippers (both pictured)
- Angled tweezers (optional)
- PVA, Weldbond glue or Titebond II Premium Wood Glue
- A selection of tiles
- A shallow dish or lid
- Grout (see Chapter 9)

Tools and glue to make the Bardo fish.

## Method:
Start by choosing your colour scheme. In this exercise we are not aiming to make an exact copy of the fish. I have used a range of Winckelmans unglazed ceramic tiles which come in natural, muted colours which are ideal for the fishy tones. The main thing to think about is the balance of lights and darks. Here, you can see that the fish has a dark upper body and detail around the gills. The middle of the fish is mostly in mid tones, and the bottom half is lighter colours. As a mosaic artist, you do not have access to the range of colours available to a painter, but by mixing colours you can give the impression of natural irregularities. You are not aiming to be 'true' to nature but to provide enough for the eye to immediately recognise what you are depicting.

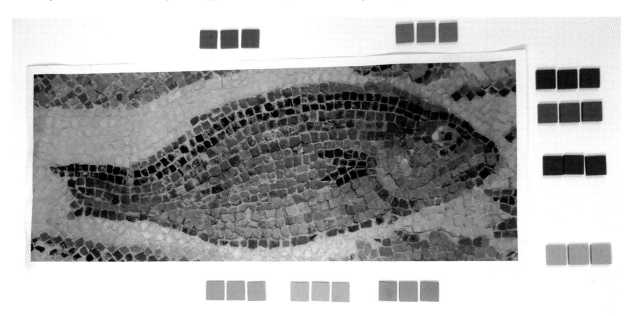

**Choose your colour scheme.**

1. Resize your fish on a photocopier and transfer your mosaic design on to the front of the board using carbon paper. Masking tape on the corners will prevent the design and carbon paper from moving around.

2. The photocopy of the fish is slightly smaller than the size of the board, so I am checking the position of the fish in relation to the edge of the board before I transfer it. For

**Transfer the design on to the board using carbon paper.**

'traditional' mosaic work, I use tesserae around 10mm square (a quarter of the 200mm square Winckelmans tiles) and as far as possible I want to avoid using slivers to fill the spaces.

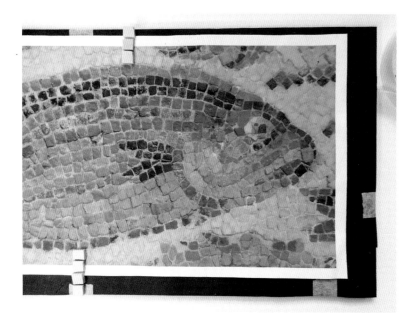

The importance of checking the spacing between your design elements, as well as between those elements and the edges of the board, cannot be stressed enough. As an example, this is a design adapted from a detail of two pears taken from an ancient floor mosaic found near Corinth in Greece. I have simplified the design and been careful during

**Think about the spacing between the fish and the edges of the board.**

the planning stage to consider the spacing at points A, B, C and D to avoid using slivers as much as possible. Consider potentially awkward spots when designing a mosaic – avoiding them at this stage will save a lot of time later.

3. Start with the main focal point of the design, in this case the eye of the fish. I cut and 'dry' lay small sections of the mosaic before I glue.

**Start with the focal point of the design.**

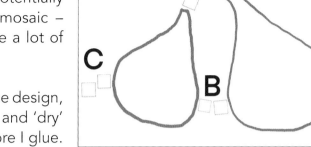

**Pear design adapted to allow for correct spacing.**

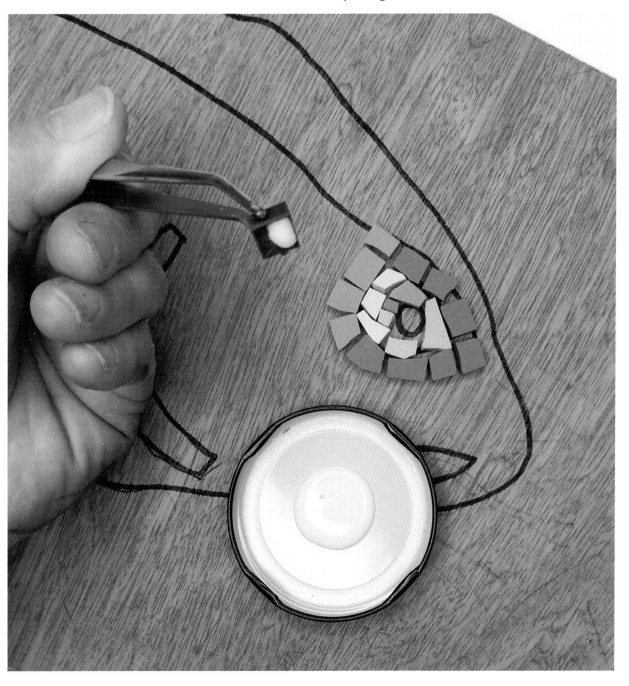

There are many ways to make a mosaic eye. Do not be tempted to put a circle down and think the job is done. It is worth spending time on this part of the mosaic to get it right. The whole mosaic will flow more smoothly if you get key features right.

**Different styles of mosaic eyes.**

4. Remember: the glue dries fairly quickly so remove any excess glue that squishes out from under the tesserae using a sharp pick. Dried glue will obstruct the placement of the adjacent tesserae.

**Remove excess glue with a sharp pick as you work.**

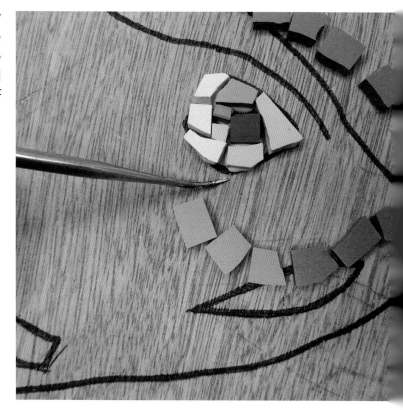

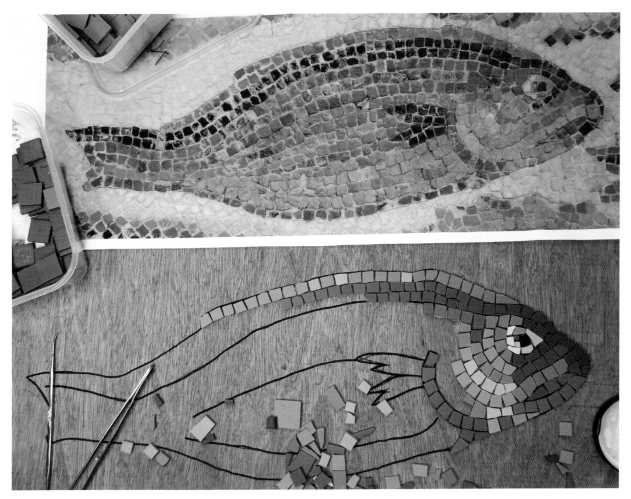

**Carry on building up the image of the fish.**

5. Carry on building up the image of the fish, moving from the head back down the length of the body. You can use the original photocopy as a guide but try not to slavishly follow it.

6. The original fish is one of a countless number of swimming creatures in a huge floor. Making a single fish to be viewed up close requires a different approach. Our particular Roman fish does not have a speckled body, but I have added speckles to provide more interest and a sense of 'realism'.

**Adding speckles to the fish's body.**

**First lay a single line of tesserae around the form of the fish and check your spacing.**

7. Once the fish is complete, start to lay a single line of tesserae in the background colour around the outline of the fish. If there are fiddly bits (such as the webbed feet of a duck or the branches of a tree) then it is not necessary to go around every crook and corner of the design, just follow the main outline. When you get close to the border, it is advisable to check your spacing to make sure that you can use whole pieces as much as possible.

Note that the background is not composed of one colour but various light tones of cream and a bit of grey. This is called peppering and helps give depth and interest to the background.

I have decided to use opus musivum in the background, in other words to create radiating lines around the fish, like ripples in a pond. This is a common way of laying the background when a sense of movement is required.

8. Always think about the piece/s which will follow from the one you have just placed. Here you can see that I am in danger of creating an almost straight outline around the fish, halting the sense of movement in the animal. However, by slightly tilting Tessera A upwards, I can create a curve in the line which will maintain the movement in the radiating circles around the fish.

**Always think about the pieces which will follow the one you have just placed.**

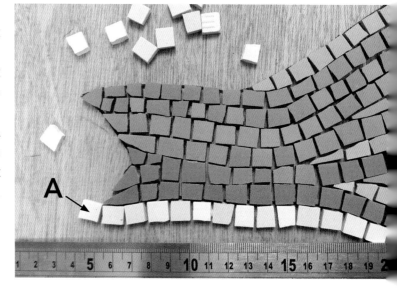

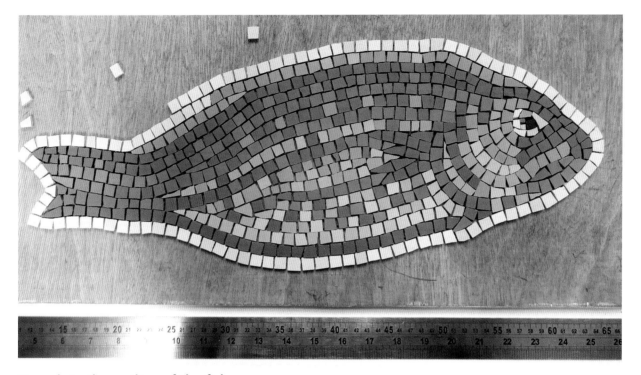

**Complete the outline of the fish.**

9. Complete the outline of the fish in the background colour/s.

10. Next lay the framing tesserae around the outer edge of the board. Make sure you have whole pieces in the corners. When you get near to the corners, place whole pieces and work inwards.

**Lay the framing tesserae.**

**Recognising trouble spots ahead.**

11. No matter how careful you have been about your spacing, you will still invariably encounter trouble spots. I need to make slight adjustments to the size of the tesserae here to avoid creating a narrow space to fill. Avoid sudden changes of size in the tesserae as far as possible.

12. Keep filling in the background and then leave the mosaic to dry for at least 24 hours before grouting (see Chapter 9).

**Completed and grouted fish.**

# CHAPTER 8:

# HOUSE NUMBER

## WINCKELMANS UNGLAZED CERAMIC AND GLASS ON WEDI BOARD

Now that you are more familiar with the fundamental principles of mosaic making, let's apply the same principles to a contemporary project – a house number on Wedi board. Wedi board is a lightweight compressed foam board which is used to line bathrooms. A similar product is called Jackoboard. Both can be bought as large panels from kitchen and bathroom suppliers. The board is covered with a thin layer of concrete with compressed foam inside and makes a superb mosaic substrate because it is suitable for outdoors and wet conditions.

The sheets come in different thicknesses and can be cut down to the required size using a Stanley or utility knife. Simply place a metal ruler along the line you wish to cut and run the knife against the ruler, scoring the surface of the board. After a few times, the thin concrete coating will split, and it is then easy to snap the board open and cut through the back.

**Note:** One disadvantage of the board is that it cannot take a lot of weight. If you are using a whole panel of the board, you will need to support it with a frame. Also, the panels are only available in certain sizes (eg: 1200mm x 600mm) so it does not suit all mosaic projects.

This project is made on 4mm thick Wedi board and measures 28cm square. The design was created digitally and then printed out to the correct size – the lazy person's option – and traced on to the board using carbon paper (see Chapter 7). I am using thin board for this project because I will attach the mosaic to the wall with outdoor-grade tile adhesive. However, if you intend to hang the mosaic you need to attach hanging fittings to the board *before* you start mosaicking (see Chapter 2). One D-ring is enough for a small work like this. For larger mosaics, two is advisable.

**Materials:**
- Piece of Wedi or Jackoboard
- Stanley or utility knife
- Metal ruler
- Mosaic design
- Carbon paper
- Pencil
- Sharpie/marker pen
- Weldbond glue or Titebond II Premium Wood Glue

- Side biter nippers or compound nippers and wheeled nippers if you want to mix glass with unglazed ceramic tiles.
- Angled tweezers (optional)
- A selection of Winckelmans and vitreous glass tiles
- Grout. I used BAL Micromax II Wall and Flour Grout for joints from 1mm to 20mm in Smoke.
- Tile adhesive. I used Mapei Adesilex P10

**Method:**

1. Go over the traced design with a Sharpie or marker pen to ensure the lines are clearly visible.

**Go over the traced design with a Sharpie.**

2. Start laying your tesserae – always start with the main focal point of the design, in this case the number itself. The ridged side of the tile is the reverse, so it is the side which is glued down. Each of the pieces used to make the numerals are cut to size to fit the space – there is no shortcut for this.

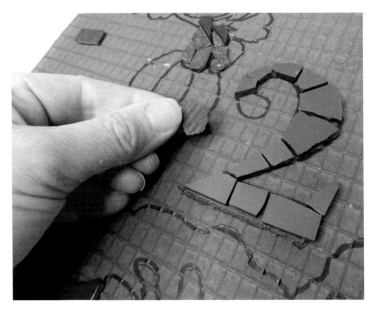

**The ridged side is placed down.**

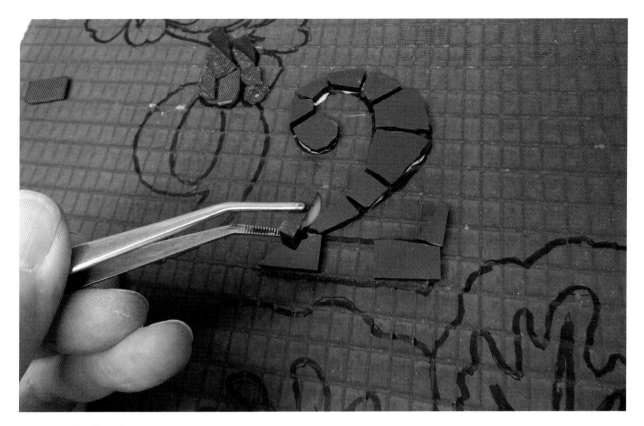

**Apply a little glue at a time.**

3. Apply a little bit of glue at a time, either holding the tessera between finger and thumb and dipping it into the glue or holding the tessera with tweezers.

4. Make adjustments to the order of work as needed. The main principle is to start with the focal point and build up from there, but on a small mosaic like this parts of the design overlap – e.g., the flower with the numerals. Also, there are places where it is wise to fill the gaps before the glue dries, such as between the numerals. This is because it will make placing the tiles in the tight spot between the numerals easier if you still have some movement with the glue. The same applies to the framing tesserae.

5. Carry on building up the design. Although this is a contemporary piece, you can see that the same principles of laying are being applied as with the Bardo fish in Chapter 7 – the tesserae

**Make adjustments to the order of work as needed.**

**Carry on building up the design.**

are offset to avoid grids and crosses and sdoppiamento or the splitting of the line is used where needed.

6. As with the Bardo fish, take care about the spacing. Your aim is to keep the size of the tesserae fairly consistent (see Learning from the Ancients, Chapter 6), so if you placed Tesserae A and B without considering the space between them, you would end up with an awkward narrow gap to fill.

**Take care about spacing.**

7. You can make both A and B slightly larger to fill the gap, but this creates another tricky space at Point C. The fundamental nature of mosaic is that the laying of each piece influences the pieces around it, so you need to keep adjusting so that all the pieces fit appropriately. Enlarging the tessera which my tool is touching will solve the problem.

**Each tessera affects the ones around it.**

**Enlarge this tessera.**

8. Now you have a nice area to fill which will not require using slivers.

**Now you have a nice area to fill.**

9. Carry on filling in the background. I like to have lively movement in the background, so I choose to create radiating lines which follow the curviest parts of the design.

**Carry on filling in the background.**

10. Leave the mosaic to dry for 24 hours and then grout it according to the instructions given in Chapter 9. When you are ready to install, make sure the surface is clean and dry and mark off the area with masking tape to keep the adjoining area clean. Spread outdoor-grade tile adhesive over the surface using a notched trowel.

11. Press the mosaic carefully into the tile adhesive and hold in place for a

**Prepare the area for the mosaic to be installed.**

Installed house number mosaic.

few minutes until it is firmly embedded. Take some excess adhesive on the end of your forefinger and run it around the outside of the mosaic, covering the sides of the board. Remove the masking tape.

# CHAPTER 9:
# GROUTING AND FINISHING

WHEN MAKING A DIRECT method mosaic on a firm substrate such as wood or compressed foam board which involves sticking the pieces to the surface with glue, you will need to grout the completed work. The grout fills up the gaps between the tesserae. Mosaics which are made on mesh (see Chapter 10) or using the face tape method (Chapter 12) will also need grouting.

**Light, mid and dark grout on identical colour boards of mixed ceramic and glass.**

However, other mosaics made using the tile adhesive (thinset mortar) method (Chapters 13–15) do not need grouting because the tesserae are held in place by the adhesive paste. Mosaics which are made in reverse and cast in concrete (Chapter 11) also do not require grouting.

The first thing you need to think about when grouting your mosaic is what colour to choose. The grout changes the mosaic – the addition of a new colour, even a muted one, alters the overall effect of the piece. First consider how light or dark your tesserae are and choose a grout colour that is similar to the tones of your tiles. For example, largely light tiles will work well with a white grout, whereas dark tones will suit a darker one.

Here, a set of three identical panels has been grouted in white, mid-grey and a dark grey. As you can see, the grout colour has a profound effect on the perceived colours of the tesserae.

When it comes to grout, I tend to err on the side of caution and mostly use a mid-grey because a bad grout decision can ruin hours of work or will involve taking steps to remedy the mistake. If you are unsure about your colour, make and grout a small test mosaic to be sure that the colour you have chosen is going to work.

Do you need to seal your mosaic first? Only if the material you are using is porous. Winckelmans unglazed ceramic tiles are not porous so they do not require sealing. However, any natural material like stone or marble must be sealed before grouting. Try LTP Mattstone, a product which can be found online or through tiling suppliers which sell stone tiles.

**Materials to grout a mosaic.**

Prepare yourself and your work area before you start grouting. Grout is a cement-based compound and mixing grout is messy, so wear an apron or an old shirt and cover the work surface with newspapers or a plastic sheet.

## MATERIALS:
- Soft brush, a clean domestic paint brush is fine
- Rubber gloves
- Dust mask
- Two deep plastic bowls or buckets. Old ice cream containers are fine for smaller mosaics
- A spreading tool. An old plastic loyalty card is ideal for small mosaics, or you can buy spreading tools at any hardware shop
- A good, thick tiler's sponge/old newspaper
- Grout. I use BAL Micromax II Wall and Flour Grout for joints from 1mm to 20mm in Smoke. Check the width of your gaps between your tesserae before you buy the grout. If your mosaic is going to be outdoors, then also be sure to choose a grout which specifies that it is suitable for wet conditions
- A large spoon or implement to mix the grout. For larger quantities of grout, use a margin trowel
- A bottle/jug of water
- Water mister, not essential but handy so that you can fine tune the amount of water you add
- A hard scrubbing brush

## Method:
1. Brush the front of the mosaic with a clean paint brush to make sure it is free of dust and particles. It helps to give the mosaic a shake too to make sure all the tesserae are firmly stuck.

2. Wearing rubber gloves and a dust mask, mix the grout according to the instructions on the packet in one of your large bowls. If possible, do this outdoors.

Add the water slowly – it will start to become granulated.

Aim for a peanut butter-like paste.

Be careful to add the water slowly – you are aiming for a peanut butter-like paste, without water sitting on the top. Use the mister to control how much water you add. If you lift a blob of grout on to the spoon it should take a second or two to drop. Once mixed, leave the grout to slake (settle) for five minutes.

3. Apply the grout to the front of the mosaic pushing it down firmly inbetween the gaps with the spreading tool. Be sure to cover the whole mosaic. Use your finger to cover the sides of the mosaic.

**Spread the grout over the surface of the mosaic.**

**Continue until all the gaps are filled.**

4. Remove all the excess grout with the spreading tool and replace it in the grout bowl.

5. If grouting a glass mosaic, then you can use scrunched up newspaper to clean the surface of the mosaic from here on. Otherwise, follow the instructions below.

6. Fill your second tub with clean water. Soak the sponge in the water and then squeeze out *every last drop* so the sponge is damp but not wet. Wipe the front of the mosaic with the sponge – once – and then turn the sponge and using a clean side, wipe the mosaic again. It's vital to always use a clean side of the sponge as otherwise you are just smearing grout residue over the cleaned parts of your work.

**Use your finger to fill the sides of the mosaic.**

Wipe the surface of the mosaic.

Freshly cleaned surface of the mosaic.

7. Keep going, frequently rinsing the sponge out and using fresh water until the front of the mosaic is clean. It will still look slightly on the grungy side, but that will come off in the final clean.

8. Leave to dry.

9. Scrub off the residue with water and the scrubbing brush. Leave to dry again.

Cleaning up properly is a critical part of grouting mosaics. No grout or grout residue should go into the drains. Leave the dirty water to settle over a number of hours and then pour away the clean surface water and wipe out the residue at the bottom of the bowl with kitchen roll or balled up newspaper.

### Trouble shooting:

If you notice little pin holes in the grout lines of your mosaic it means that your grout was too wet. Tip: always keep a bit of grout aside during the clean-up process to fill holes.

If any tiles come off during the grouting process, then do not despair. Put the loose piece to one side and carry on grouting the mosaic as normal. Once it is clean, use a sharp tool to pick out the grout that will have filled the gap left by the missing tile. Quickly dry the gap with a hairdryer, apply a touch of superglue to the back of the tile and reposition it. You will then be able to grout it with a little bit of grout on the end of your finger.

**Bad grout days.** If you decide later that you really do not like the grout colour that you have chosen, then there are ways to remedy the problem. Emma Biggs and Tessa Hunkin write in *Mosaic Patterns* (New Holland Publishers, 2006):

Apply mortar cleaner to the surface which will eat away at the grout a little leaving room for the new colour. Another way to darken the grout colour is to oil the mosaic with linseed oil. This will sink into the joints and can be washed off the surface of the tiles with a mild detergent after 15 minutes.

Alternatively, in the same book, Biggs and Hunkin suggest:

Another way to change grout colour you don't like: give the mosaic a good scratch over with a soft wire brush and regrout. It is generally easier to make a light grout dark than the other way around. Apply a light coat of the darker colour with a paint brush.

# CHAPTER 10:

# PEAR WALL PLAQUE

## WINCKELMANS UNGLAZED CERAMIC AND VITREOUS GLASS ON FIBREGLASS MESH

The mesh method for making mosaics is an alternative approach to the ordinary direct method discussed in Chapters 7 and 8. The advantage of the method is that you are not sticking the tiles on to a solid substrate but gluing them to fibreglass mesh, a close weave mesh commonly used in the tiling process.

Using this method allows you to follow the design which is clearly visible through the mesh. When the work is complete, simply lift the mesh off and apply the mosaic to its permanent surface. The fact that the mesh is malleable means that the mesh method is a good option to choose if you have a curved surface or if you want to make a large direct method mosaic and cut it into smaller sections to transport or for easier installation.

The mesh remains part of the mosaic even after installation, so it is not recommended for floors where adhesion between the tesserae and the cement surface is of paramount importance. The mesh method works best with flat, purpose-made mosaic tiles like Winckelmans and vitreous glass.

The key point to remember when making a mosaic on mesh is to be economical with the glue. You want the glue to cover the back of the tile, but not to squish out between the pieces. If it does, it will prevent the tile adhesive from pressing up from underneath the mosaic when it is installed.

**Materials:**
- Mosaic design
- Black marker or Sharpie pen
- Plain paper
- Backing board
- Cling film (Saran wrap)
- A piece of fibreglass mesh slightly larger than the size of your mosaic
- Masking tape
- Side biter nippers or compound nippers, and wheeled nippers if you want to mix Winckelmans tiles with vitreous glass
- Angled tweezers (optional)
- Outdoor-grade glue such as Weldbond or Titebond II Premium Wood Glue
- A selection of Winckelmans and vitreous glass tiles
- A 3mm notched tile adhesive comb
- Outdoor-grade tile adhesive – I use BAL Max Flex Fibre, Flexible Tile Adhesive for Walls and Floors
- Grout. I use BAL Micromax II Wall and Flour Grout for joints from 1mm to 20mm in Smoke

## Method:

1. Prepare a design for your mosaic and draw it out on to plain paper using a marker pen, then decide on your colours. Remember that strong, simple designs work best for mosaic.

**Draw out your design.**

2. Spread a layer of cling film (Saran wrap) over the design. If your mosaic is larger than the width of the film, then slightly overlap two widths of film side by side. The natural property of the film means that the overlapping edges will 'cling' together, so they do not have to be glued or taped down.

3. Make sure the cling film layer is as flat as possible with no creases or bubbles and tape it down on the back of the board with masking tape, pulling it tight as you do so. Lay a piece of mesh over the cling film and the design. Tape down the mesh with masking tape, also keeping it as flat as possible.

**Cling film and mesh spread over the design.**

**Give yourself time to think through the planning stage.**

4. By the time I had laid out the mosaic under the cling film and mesh, I had changed my mind about the colours, moving away from the orangey yellow that I was thinking about as a background colour. Changes are difficult to make when you are creating mosaics so it is best to allow yourself plenty of time to think through the planning stage and make decisions that you will be happy with.

5. Start building up the design. The unifying factor here is the rectangular shape of the tiles and the dark versus light greens. The contrast also comes from the glass for the branches and ceramic for the background.

**Start building up the design.**

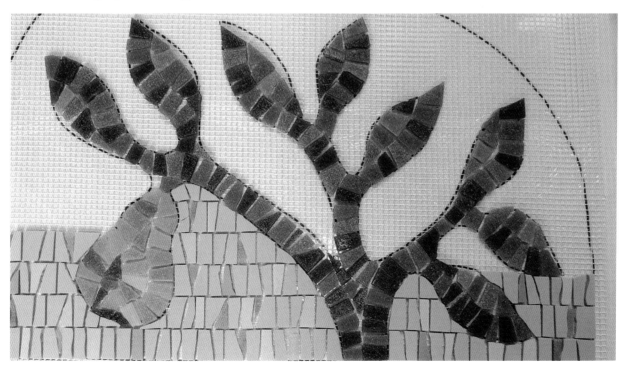

**No need for an outline.**

6. There is no need for an outline (see Chapter 7) around the shape of the design. The decision to use it or not depends on the effect you want to achieve. Having an outline would be unwieldy given that I am using rectangular tesserae.

7. During the design stage I have considered the size of the tesserae to avoid sudden size changes in the pieces (see Principle 2, in Chapter 6). Sometimes, however, these are unavoidable.

**Changes in the sizes of the pieces are sometimes unavoidable.**

**The completed mosaic is ready to install.**

**Cut the mosaic away from the excess mesh.**

8. Once the mosaic is complete, leave it to dry for 24 hours. Then you can cut it away from the excess mesh using the Stanley (utility) knife and peel away the cling film (Saran wrap) from behind.

9. Prepare the surface where you intend to install the mosaic, making sure it is dry and free from dust. Then spread outdoor tile adhesive over the surface using a 3mm notched tile adhesive comb. Winckelmans and many mosaic glass tiles are 4mm thick so the notching

**Press the mosaic into place.**

**Grouted and completed mosaic.**

on the comb ensures that the adhesive is spread evenly and does not exceed 3mm deep. Carefully place the mosaic over the adhesive and press it into place, holding it in position for a few minutes until it is secure.

It is likely that some of the adhesive will squish up between the tiles and on to the surface of the mosaic. This can easily be wiped off with a damp sponge. Leave the mosaic for 24 hours for the adhesive to set and then grout normally (see Chapter 9).

# CHAPTER 11:

# STEPPING STONE

## VITREOUS AND MEXICAN GLASS, REVERSE CAST METHOD

For this project we are making a mosaic in reverse which will be cast in concrete to create a garden stepping stone. The project involves using the indirect method on paper and the finished mosaic is suitable for outdoors. The method of working indirectly on paper is also perfect for larger projects, particularly creating mosaic for floors because it achieves

**Koi Pond Mosaic, Carterton Town Square, Oxfordshire. Gary Drostle.**

Robson Cezar, Hackney Mosaic Project volunteer, making a section of the West Hackney Recreation Ground mosaic.

a completely flat surface. It is worth looking at the work created by mosaicist Gary Drostle who uses this method for his floor mosaics.

The same method is used by the Hackney Mosaic Project, a group of volunteers based in London, UK, led by mosaicist Tessa Hunkin. The advantage of using paper as a temporary base for large-scale mosaics, particularly community work where different people are working on different parts of the mosaic at the same time, is that it can be cut and then joined together like a giant jigsaw during installation.

The only (relatively minor) disadvantage with the method is that you need to use tiles which have the same colour both front and back such as Winckelmans unglazed ceramic, glass or marble. Domestic tiles which are glazed on one side and plain on the other are not suitable because you are working in reverse and therefore you would only see the plain back of the tiles during construction. If you want to use domestic tiles, then turn to Chapter 12 for an alternative method.

The design for the stepping stone is an abstract one, loosely based on a traditional quilting pattern. Instead of cutting the tiles into squares and laying them according to the Roman mosaic principles (see Chapter 6), they are random shapes composed of squares, rectangles and triangles. The stepping stone is made entirely of glass.

**West Hackney Recreation Ground at St Paul's Church, Stoke Newington, London. Hackney Mosaic Project.** Photo: Tessa Hunkin

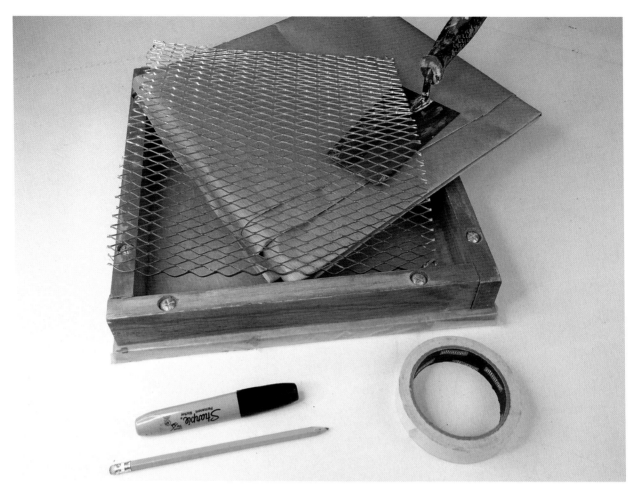

**Materials:**

- Brown Kraft paper, 60–80gsm
- Pencil
- Sharpie or marker pen
- Masking tape
- Backing board
- Plain white flour
- Glue brush
- Clean jam jar
- Mosaic materials – ceramic, glass or marble
- Stanley (utility) knife
- Dust mask
- Rubber gloves
- Casting frame, either buy one or make one with four batons and a staple gun. Lay the batons around the mosaic creating a frame – staple or tack the batons together where they join, keeping them as close together as possible
- Petroleum jelly/Vaseline
- Two mixing bowls
- Domestic paint brush
- Mixing trowel
- Cement

- Sand
- Expanded metal lath or chicken wire cut slightly smaller than the size of the mosaic
- Plastic sheeting
- Tiler's sponge
- A stiff scrubbing brush

## Method:

1. Cut the paper to the size that your mosaic is going to be, leaving a generous margin around it. Draw the design out on to the shiny side of the brown paper with pencil and then go over the pencil marks with a marker pen so that the lines can be clearly seen.

**Draw the design on to the shiny side of the brown paper.**

2. Flip the paper over so now you are working in reverse on the *matt* side of the paper. You will be able to see the marker pen lines through the paper to guide you. Tape the paper down on to your board with masking tape so that it is flat.

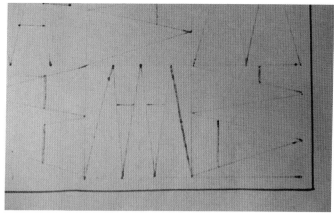

**Flip the paper over.**

3. Make a flour and water glue paste. The glue used for a reverse method mosaic on paper needs to be water soluble as the paper will be dampened and peeled off once the mosaic has been cast or set into its permanent base. To make the paste, add two to three heaped teaspoons of plain white flour to 300ml of water in a small saucepan. Heat the water gently, stirring continuously so that the flour dissolves into the water. Keep stirring until you have a thickish paste which should be firm without being solid. If it's too firm, then just add a few drops of hot water and stir. To help preservation, add half a teaspoon of salt or store in the fridge.

**Make the flour and water glue paste.**

4. Put a small amount of glue into a jar lid and put aside the rest for later. Apply your tesserae to the paper one by one reverse side up (often this is the ridged side). You are looking at the back of the mosaic – the front will be revealed later. Using a small brush, spread enough glue for four to five tesserae on to the paper and press the pieces into it. Do not use too much glue as it will make the paper wrinkle.

**Apply the glue with a small brush.**

**Carry on building up the design.**

5. Carry on building up the design. The great advantage of this method is that you are using a water-soluble glue so it is easy to correct mistakes. If you need to undo a part of the mosaic, cut out a piece of a kitchen sponge cloth the same size as the part you want to take out. Dampen it and place it under the tesserae you want to remove, pressing the tesserae down so that the paper has contact with the damp sponge. Wait a few minutes and lift the tesserae off. Wait for that section to dry naturally before re-gluing the pieces, or use a hairdryer to dry the paper quickly.

6. Once the mosaic is complete, rub petroleum jelly (Vaseline) on the inside of the frame. The grease stops the cement from sticking to the frame.

**Rub petroleum jelly around the inside of the frame.**

**Place the mosaic into the casting frame.**

7. Cut away the excess paper around the mosaic design with a Stanley (utility) knife, and place the mosaic, paper side down, tile-side up, into the casting frame.

8. Wearing rubber gloves and a dust mask, mix cement with water to make a pourable slurry in one of the mixing bowls. At the same time, mix three parts sand to one-part cement with the trowel in the second mixing bowl and add water until you have a thick consistency. It should not be runny nor too stiff.

**Cement slurry.**

**Sand and cement mixture.**

9. Using the domestic paint brush, spread the slurry on the back of the mosaic, working it quickly inbetween the tesserae until the mosaic is completely covered. The reason for making this runnier mixture is to ensure that the cement fills the gaps between the tesserae. However, the glue is water soluble so will start to dissolve when it comes into contact with water – so do this swiftly.

10. Put half of the stiff cement mixture into the mould, filling it to about halfway up the frame. Make sure the mixture gets into the corners by picking up the mould and tilting it and gently tapping it against the table. Then lay the piece of expanded metal lath on top of the cement and put the rest of the stiff cement mixture over it, completely covering the lath.

11. Wrap the mould in the sheet of plastic or lay the plastic over the mould putting weights on the corners and leave the mosaic to cure for a few days. The number of days depends on how warm it is, but no fewer than three days. When you unwrap the mould, the concrete should be solid. If you have a casting frame like this one, you can unscrew the batons and they will come away easily.

**Spread the slurry on the back of the mosaic.**

**Fill the frame halfway up and lay the expanded metal lath on top.**

**Unscrew the batons from the casting frame.**

12. Turn the mosaic over and use a sponge to dampen the paper thoroughly so that it darkens.

13. Wait at least ten minutes and then gently peel away the paper, working from the corners towards the centre. The front of the mosaic will be revealed.

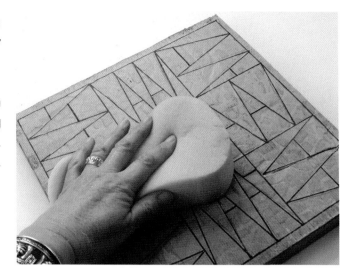

**Dampen the paper with a sponge.**

**The front of the mosaic will be revealed.**

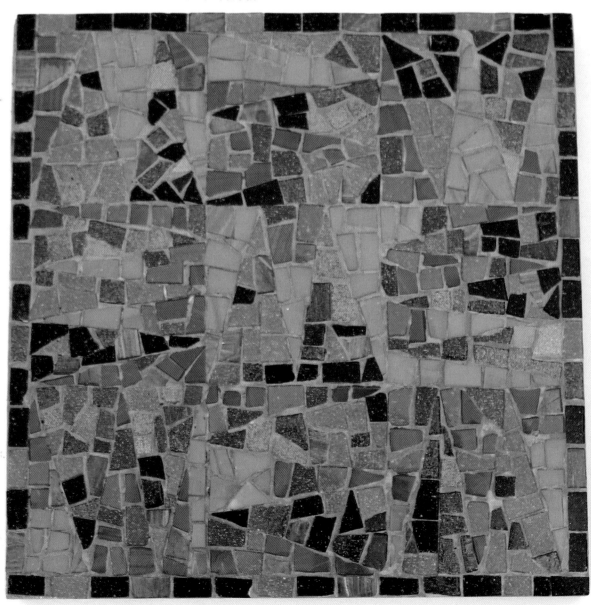

# CHAPTER 12:

# ABSTRACT WALL PANEL

## GLAZED DOMESTIC TILES, FACE TAPE METHOD

This mosaic is made using bargain basement domestic tiles which are laid directly on to a temporary sticky backing. Once the design is complete, heavy-duty tilers' 'face tape' is stuck to the *front* of the tiles. The wall is prepared with a layer of tile adhesive and the mosaic pressed into it. When the tile adhesive is dry, the face tape is peeled off and the mosaic grouted in the normal way.

The key advantage to the method is that allows you to use domestic tiles for mosaics and to work directly so that you can see the design as it emerges. It is also a good method for mosaics made of broken crockery, although to work successfully there should not be too much variation in the thickness of the tiles.

The fact that the placing of the pieces can be changed while they are still on their temporary sticky backing is an obvious plus point too. A mosaic made in this way can easily be cut into sections, stacked and moved to site, and it is a method which is perfect for both indoor and outdoor projects. If you use it for outdoors, make sure that your materials are frost proof and water resistant.

**Materials:**
- Plain paper
- Pencil
- Sharpie or marker pens
- Sticky back plastic (contact tape)
- Masking tape
- Selection of domestic tiles
- Dust mask
- Flat bed tile cutter
- Side biter nippers or compound nippers
- Half-round tile file
- Tilers' face tape
- Ground sheet/newspapers
- Tile adhesive, checking it is suitable for outdoors if necessary
- Mixing bowl
- Mixing trowel
- Tile adhesive, I used Mapei Adesilex P10
- Tile adhesive comb
- Grout float
- Grout. For this mosaic I used BAL Micromax 2 Wall and Floor Grout in Antique White.

## Method:

1. Make a template of the area where the mosaic will be installed and draw a clear line around the perimeter of the template with a marker pen. Make sure that this perimeter line is precisely drawn. If you are installing the mosaic in a specific space, you need it to fit neatly. If you are following a design, then draw it on to the template with pencil and then draw over the pencil lines with marker pen.

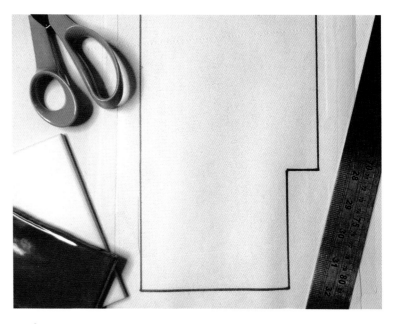

**Make a template and cover it with sticky back plastic.**

This mosaic is a simple abstract design using the changing size of the key elements to create interest, so I did not need to pre-draw it on to the template. The colour palette is limited to shades of green with pops of yellow on a white background.

Lay the template on a flat surface and cover it with sticky back plastic (contact tape), taping it down with masking tape.

2. Cut a random selection of half and quarter-sized tiles using the flat bed tile cutter. To use the cutter, lay the tile into the cutter so that is firmly placed against the end. Lower the handle so that the cutting wheel is in contact with the tile and then push the handle away from you so that the cutter scores the tile. This should be done in one smooth movement. Then lift the handle so that the built-in tile snapper is on top of the score line. Press down lightly with the handle and the tile will snap.

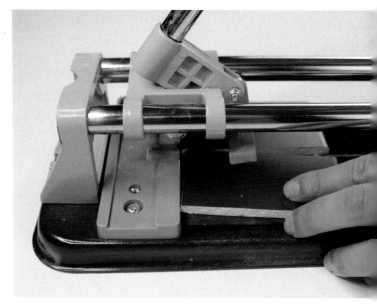

**Cut a selection of tiles with the flatbed tile cutter.**

3. Cut a good pile of smaller pieces with the flat bed tile cutter as well as shapes with the side biter nippers so that you have plenty to choose from and then start building up your design on the sticky paper. Ragged edges on the tiles can be filed back with a half-round tile file. Wear a dust mask while filing.

**Tip:** Don't cut tiles near the sticky paper because the dust will decrease its adhesion.

**Start building up the design.**

**Lay the tiler's tape over the front of the tiles.**

4. The mosaic uses the opus paladanium style of laying, a crazy paving effect where you are fitting random shaped pieces together like a jigsaw. Use a metal ruler to check that the edges are straight and keep within the perimeter line. As far as possible, lay the smooth manufactured edges of the tiles along the edge of the mosaic. Once the mosaic is complete, lay the tiler's tape over the front of the tiles, pressing it down firmly.

5. When the tape is firmly attached, it is easy to lift up sections of the mosaic and move them out of the way. Number the backs of the sections and put an arrow to indicate which way up it goes to facilitate piecing the mosaic jigsaw together at the installation stage.

**Lift up sections of the mosaic.**

**Fit the pieces of the mosaic together in their final positions.**

**Tamp the tiles with a grout float.**

6. When it's time for installation, prepare the tile adhesive and spread it over the surface where the mosaic is going, using a notched trowel to make a smooth bed. Then carefully fit the pieces of the mosaic together in their final positions, sliding them into place. The face tape is still on the surface of the tiles at this stage.

7. Tamp the mosaic firmly into the tile adhesive with a grout float and leave to dry.

8. When the adhesive is thoroughly dry you can peel off the face tape and grout the mosaic in the normal way (see Chapter 9).

eel off the face tape.

The completed mosaic.

# CHAPTER 13:

# BEACH WALK MOSAIC

## FOUND AND RECYCLED MATERIALS, TILE ADHESIVE METHOD

From this chapter onwards, we are going to be examining an entirely different way of making mosaics. The method does not entail using conventional glue and no grouting is involved. It is called the tile adhesive or thinset mortar method and consists of pressing the tesserae into a thick paste.

**Mosaic 'virus'. Shells, mirrored glass, single-use plastics from diabetic needles, vitreous glass, beach-foraged ceramic, brick and more. Helen Miles.**

The wonderful thing about this method is that you can use tesserae of different thicknesses so the choice of items to include is almost limitless: from pebbles to broken plates, junk jewellery and beads, buttons, rocks, bottle tops, shells, dried seeds, coins, keys, discarded plastics such as cutlery, broken toys and medical waste, scraps from other mosaic projects, nails/screws/nuts/bolts and any other things that you can think of and happen to find in the back of a drawer.

The only caveat is that it helps if the items are not too thick or heavy, have at least one flattish surface and that they can be easily cut or broken down into smaller parts when needed (but this last requirement is not essential). I can guarantee you one thing – the next time you break a favourite mug, your heart will sing!

If you intend to install your mosaic outdoors then make sure that your items will withstand the weather conditions – the patterns on transfer ware crockery, for example, will peel off if exposed to frost.

The only disadvantage of the method is that it can be messy and you have to be aware of the adhesive's drying time. Tile adhesive is a cement-based compound and starts to harden, albeit slowly, as soon as you mix it with water, so take care to clean away excess adhesive if you stop working.

**Efflorescence caused by working in cold conditions.**

Also be aware that in cold conditions, a white bloom, or effloresence, can appear on the surface of the adhesive once it has dried. To prevent this, work in reasonably warm conditions and use an admixture when you mix the tile adhesive.

This mosaic is made using a variety of materials, including sea glass and pebbles collected on a beach walk with an old friend.

**Materials:**
- Your choice of tesserae
- A base – marine plywood, MDF, tile backer board such as Hardie backer, compressed foam board (Wedi or Jackoboard) or a home-made fibreglass mesh and thinset mortar substrate (see Chapter 2)
- Sharpie or marker pen
- Plain paper
- Sticky back plastic/contact paper
- Apron or old shirt
- Newspaper or a plastic sheet to cover your work area

- Dust mask
- Single-use gloves. These are not ideal for environmental reasons but it is hard to avoid using them as normal rubber gloves do not give you enough fine control. However, I prefer not to wear gloves and just wipe my hands when I get adhesive on them
- Tile adhesive/thinset mortar. I use BAL Max Flex Fibre, Flexible Tile Adhesive for Walls and Floors
- Black mortar tone/pigment
- Admixture, optional
- Ziplock plastic food storage bag
- Plastic tub for mixing adhesive – an old yoghurt pot or icecream tub is perfect
- Old spoon
- Spatula
- Side biter nippers or compound nippers. Wheeled nippers are useful too
- Angled tweezers
- Wet rag

**Method:**

1. Make sure your materials are clean and dry – shells and sea pebbles need to be throughly washed to remove salt residue. The best way to do this is to soak them in fresh water over a number of days, changing the water daily.

**Experiment with your materials.**

2. Sort, organise and cut your materials into usable sizes as much as possible before you start work. This is because the adhesive starts to set once it is mixed so you want to spend as little time as possible cutting and preparing your materials during the laying stage.

3. Begin by experimenting with your materials, seeing what works well together by moving them into different positions. Nothing is being stuck at this stage so this is the time to play and make sure you are happy with the combination of materials.

There are many different approaches to making a mosaic abstract:

- Taking a favourite piece such as part of a broken tea cup or shells from a holiday into the central point and then building the mosaic around it.
- Putting dark colours in the centre or the bottom of the piece and gradually working out to lighter colours, or visa versa. Using different shapes or textures to create contrast and patterns.
- Changing the spacing of your pieces. Some could be closely spaced, but you could lay them further apart as the mosaic grows, or alternate tight with loose spacing.
- Exploring the reflectivity of your pieces. Some might be shiny and others more matt. The shinier ones, especially if they have bright colours, will be more prominent in the piece so use them accordingly.
- Experimenting with the different sides of the tesserae – if you are using scraps from other mosaic projects you can try putting flat tiles on their sides or at an angle and can use the ridged backs of the tesserae to create interesting texture.

**Do a partial dry lay to check you are happy with the composition.**

4. Although others prefer to dive right in, I like to prepare a rough plan of the mosaic before I mix the adhesive. Do this by drawing a circle on to a piece of plain paper approximately the same size as your intended mosaic and divide it into four quadrants, numbering each one. This is to help you keep track of where the pieces 'belong' when you transpose them into the adhesive.

Lay a piece of sticky back plastic (contact paper) over the paper circle and create the mosaic using the sticky paper to hold the pieces in place. The advantage of the sticky paper is that it allows you to lay a trial version of the mosaic, making adjustments without having to dig out adhesive. However, be aware that once you start moving the pieces into the adhesive bed, the precise configuation of the pieces will be lost.

**Create a rough plan of the mosaic using sticky paper.**

When I'm ready to start setting the tesserae into the adhesive. I will constantly be making changes and adjustments as I work, but this is the plan.

**The planned mosaic.**

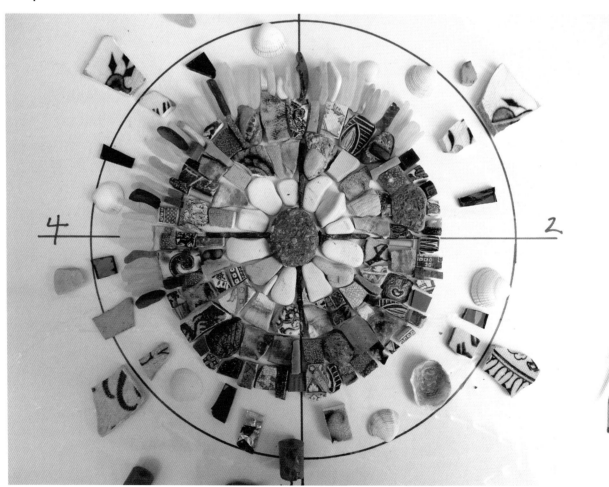

**Draw the circle and guide lines on to the base.**

5. Draw the same sized circle and guide lines on to your base using a Sharpie pen.

6. Wearing a dust mask, add dry black pigment (if you are using) to the dry tile adhesive. Aim for a pigment to adhesive ratio of no more than 10 per cent. Put the powdered mix into a ziplock bag – there should be enough in the bag for the entire project. Take about three heaped tablespoons of the same mixture from the bag and put it into a plastic tub; add water slowly until you have a thick paste, like peanut butter.

7. Take a small quantity of this paste (enough for the initial tesserae) and spread a thin layer, or 'scratch coat' onto the centre of the board with the back of the pointed end of your spatula. Take a larger quantity of the paste to create a bed thick enough to hold

**Prepare the tile adhesive, adding mortar tone or pigment if required.**

the tesserae half to two-thirds of the way up. If you find it difficult to manipulate the adhesive, another approach is to put a small quantity in the bottom corner of a food storage bag and nip off the corner so that you can squeeze out the adhesive like frosting on a cake; either way make sure that there is good contact between the adhesive and the substrate.

**Spread adhesive on to the board and start transposing the pieces.**

8. As you place the pieces into the adhesive, try to avoid the adhesive squishing up, creating a raised ridge around them. Sometimes it is easier to place them using angled tweezers. Keep a wet rag nearby so that you can keep wiping your fingers and/or tweezers to avoid getting any adhesive on the tesserae. If you do get adhesive on the pieces then you can remove the piece, wipe and re-lay. However, sometimes it is easier to discard the piece and find another.

9. **Tip:** If you want to add sea glass to your mosaic, be aware that the coloured adhesive under the glass will absorb and dull the translucency of the

**Continue to build up the design.**

material. This mosaic includes a ring of sea glass set on its edge. One half of the ring is set into black adhesive (left) and the other half in white (right) to show the difference.

10. Another great advantage of the tile adhesive method is that space can be left between the areas of tesserae as a deliberate design feature.

Sea glass in the tile adhesive.

**Consider leaving parts of the mosaic untessallated.**

CHAPTER 14:

# PIQUE ASSIETTE BIRD

## BROKEN TABLE WARE, TILE ADHESIVE METHOD

Pique Assiette is a particular style of mosaic which uses broken ceramics to make designs. The name derives from the French for 'thief of plates' and is said to have originated with Raymond Isidore, a road worker and cemetery caretaker, who created the famous Maison Picassiette in Chartres, France in the early twentieth century. Pique Assiette is a popular way to repurpose tableware.

The beauty of Pique Assiette is the unexpected combination of patterns and colours which comes from mixing different fragments in one design. Pique Assiette mosaics often include much larger pieces than other types of mosaics and the selection, cutting and positioning of the pieces is critical to the effectiveness of the work.

For this project we are going to make a Pique Assiette bird on a machine-cut MDF substrate. Hardie backer, Wedi or Jackoboard, slate or a terracotta pot would also make

**Roundel detail from the Pique Assiette House, Chartres, France.**

**Orchid on slate. Broken china, millefiori, vitreous and stained glass. Rhona Duffy.**

suitable substrates for a project like this. If using wood or terracotta, prime it first with a coat of PVA/water mix (see below).

**Materials:**
- MDF substrate, these can be bought pre-cut or cut at home with a jigsaw
- Medium grade sandpaper
- Stanley or utility knife
- PVA glue
- Domestic paint brush
- MDF wood primer and paint
- Dust mask
- Safety glasses
- Latex gripper gloves
- A selection of plates
- Side biter or compound nippers and wheeled nippers if using thinner china
- Hammer
- Old towel
- Bucket
- Sticky back plastic/contact paper
- Tile adhesive. I use BAL Max Flex Fibre, Flexible Tile Adhesive for Walls and Floors
- Mortar tone/pigment, black
- Spatula
- Mixing pot, an old yoghurt pot is fine
- Angled tweezers (optional)
- Wet rag

**Method:**

1. Prime and paint the back of the board and the edges. This is best done before you start mosaicking to avoid getting paint on the mosaic.

2. Prepare the side of the board which will be mosaicked by rubbing with sandpaper then scoring the surface in a criss-cross pattern with the Stanley (utility) knife. Then combine PVA glue and water in a 50:50 ratio, stirring until the glue has dissolved into the water. Brush the gluey water over the front of the mosaic and leave to dry.

3. Take time to select and sort your mosaic materials. As with other types of mosaic, the success of Pique Assiette depends on having good contrast between the different

**Select and cut your materials in advance.**

materials. This can be achieved in a number of ways, including by using bright colours beside dull ones, light tones against dark, patterned plates with plain ones and so on.

4. Wearing latex gripper gloves, safety glasses and a dust mask, cut your materials so that you have a selection to choose from as you work. The type of hand tool you will use depends on the type of ceramic you are cutting – thinner bone china will cut with wheeled Leponitt nippers, whereas thicker crockery will need side biters or compound nippers. If you want to achieve precision cuts, you will need to use a Dremel or an electric wet saw. Sometimes it is easier to start by putting the plate under a towel and hitting it with a hammer and then refine the cuts from there. To prevent flying shards, cut into a bucket.

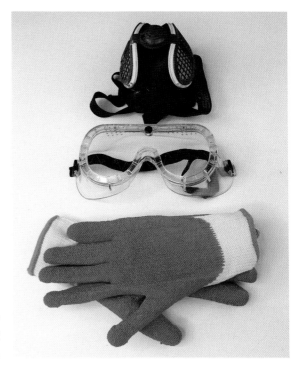

Pique Assiette mosaics are stuck with tile adhesive (see Chapter 13) which starts to set as soon as it is mixed with water, so it is important to do as much preparation as possible before you begin laying. I like to lay out my pre-cut pieces on to a template covered with sticky

**Safety equipment.**

back plastic (see Chapter 13) before mixing the adhesive, so everything is prepared in advance.

5. Prepare the tile adhesive (see Chapter 13), adding mortar tone if desired and spread a small amount on to the substrate. Remember to always work on a small section at a time

**Pieces selected and cut and laid onto sticky back plastic before sticking.**

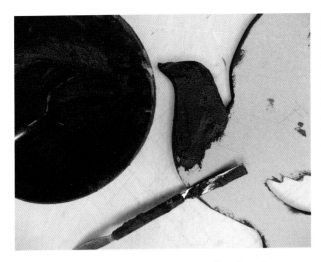

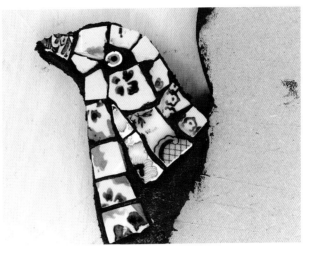

**Only spread a small amount of adhesive at a time.**

**Lay the tesserae according to your pre-cut plan.**

and to remove excess adhesive from around the laid pieces. Start at the focal point of a mosaic design – here it is the eye which is a single piece of millefiori.

6. Best practice is to keep wiping the tips of your tweezers (if using) and your fingers with a wet rag as you work so that you don't get the adhesive on to the surface of the ceramic. Continue to build up the design. Once one row has been laid, it is easier to lay the subsequent ones using the first as the guide. If you need to stop, remove all excess adhesive. Otherwise, it will harden and obstruct you from laying subsequent pieces.

**Continue to build up the design.**

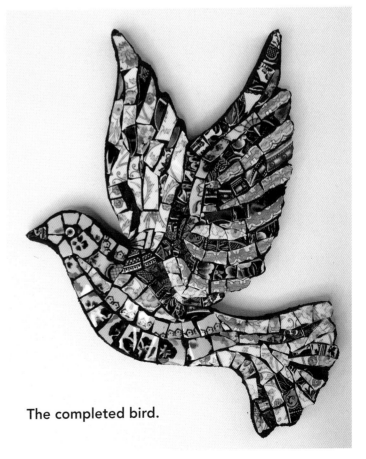

**The completed bird.**

# CHAPTER 15:
# DECORATED BALLS

## FOUND AND RECYCLED MATERIALS ON POLYSTYRENE BALLS, TILE ADHESIVE METHOD

You only need to think of Antoni Gaudi's mosaics decorating the curving walls of parks and public buildings in Barcelona, Spain, to realise that surfaces for mosaics don't have to be flat. Mosaic artists love to decorate three-dimensional surfaces whether by making their own sculptures and mosaicking over them or using easy to find, ready-made objects as bases for their work.

**Christmas and Easter decorated balls.**

This pot (right) was made using Cesi ceramic tiles and mirrored glass which were glued directly on to the surface and grouted. For extra strength and frost proof durability, the inside and bottom of the pot was painted with one layer of epoxy paint prior to applying the tesserae on the outside.

Helen Nock (below) makes eco bricks out of empty water bottles and other containers which are stuffed with soft plastic wrappings that would otherwise go into landfill. To make this horse, she tied discarded containers together to make the basic proportions of the animal. Helen encased it in chicken wire, before mummifying the form in strips of material dipped in cement slurry the consistency of double cream. The structure was then mosaicked over.

The ingenuity of mosaic artists seeking to create three-dimensional forms for their work knows no limits. Joy Parker created a substrate by using an old metal lamp as an armature and then built up the form in a similar way to Helen Nock.

**Marigold summer pot. Wilma van der Meyden.**

**Horse, work in progress. Plastic bottles and tubing encased in chicken wire. Helen Nock.**

**The completed structure is then mosaicked. Helen Nock.**

Head. Smalti, sea glass and pebbles. Joy Parker.

However, you don't have to make your own substrates to create interesting three-dimensional mosaics. Terracotta planters, old chimney pots, wooden furniture and concrete garden bird baths and columns, are all great options for mosaic substrates. Remember that wood needs to be prepared and that any non-mosaicked wooden surfaces should be coated with yacht varnish if they are intended for continuous outdoor use. Other than that, you're good to go.

This project uses polystyrene balls and egg shapes to create Christmas and Easter decorations with foraged and recycled materials.

## Materials:
- Plasticine or clay
- Barbeque wooden skewers
- Polystyrene balls and eggs. I used 9cm and 10cm eggs and 5cm and 9cm balls
- Primer. I use BAL All in One Bonding Agent, Primer and Admixture
- Paint brush, 3–5cm
- Galvanised staples, you can use metal paint to colour these
- Felt tip pen, optional
- Dust mask
- Wire cutters
- Side biter or compound nippers and wheeled nippers
- Tile adhesive. I use BAL Max Flex Fibre, Flexible Tile Adhesive for Walls and Floors
- Mortar tone/pigment, black
- Spatula
- Mixing bowl
- Angled tweezers
- Wet rag
- A number of thin-necked jam jars

## Method:

1. Create little mounds out of the plasticine or clay, stick the skewers into the bottom of the balls and then into the mound to hold the balls in place. Then coat the balls with a layer of primer and leave to dry.

**Coat the balls with a layer of primer.**

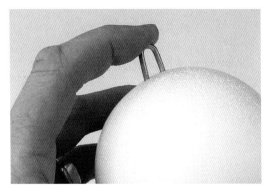

**Push galvanised staples into the balls.**

2. Push galvanised staples into the top of the balls

3. Sort, organise and cut your mosaic materials. This ball was made using non-recyclable plastic waste, including dried up felt tip pens, folded aluminium blister packs, diabetes syringe covers, plastic straws, the lid of a pot noodle, the neck of a tube of moisturizer, millefiori and the odd bit of rolled tin can found squashed in the road. Decent wire cutters will cut easily through ordinary household waste like this.

**Ball made with non-recyclable plastic waste.**

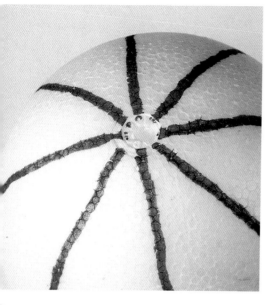

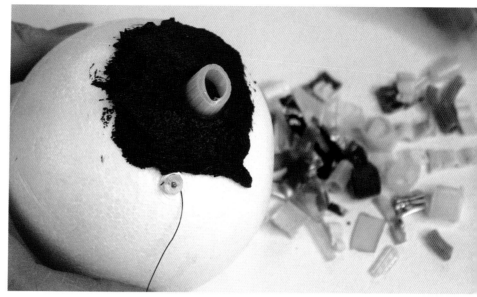

**Draw guidelines on to the ball with a felt tip pen.**

**Spread a little adhesive and press your materials into it.**

4. If needed, draw guidelines on the balls with a felt tip pen. This is helpful if you want to change colours or use different materials on different segments.

5. Mix tile adhesive and mortar tone as set out in Chapter 13. Spread a little adhesive on to the top part of the ball and begin pressing your materials into it. The normal rule is that the adhesive should cover half to two-thirds of the items to hold them securely, but lightweight plastics like these require less adhesive. Continue adding bits one by one making sure that they are firmly embedded. Use angled tweezers if necessary.

6. Once half of the ball is complete, carefully scrape away the excess adhesive and leave it to dry overnight on the top of narrow-rimmed jam jars. The lighter balls can stay on their barbeque skewers.

**Complete half and then leave to dry.**

7. Once the first half is thoroughly dry, you can mosaic the other half of the decorations.

The fun thing about these balls is that you can use all kinds of unusual materials and experiment. Among other things, I included an old mug with lettering, brick collected on the beach, mirrored glass, fragments of glass and ceramic from other mosaic projects, millefiori and a nail. You can change the shape of your tesserae, flip them over to use the side which is normally downwards and play with unexpected positionings.

**Mosaic the other half of the decoration.**

**Mosaicked balls.**

# GLOSSARY

**Andamento.** Traditionally used to refer to the internal flow or movement of the lines that constitute the work. The word is also used to refer to the process of building up lines of tesserae within contemporary mosaic work.

**Interstices.** The spaces between the tesserae.

**Opus (singular), opera (plural), opuses also used.** The direct translation from Latin is 'work'. In this context it means the different patterns used to fill in the background of a mosaic. See Chapter 6.

**Sdoppiamento:** The splitting and re-merging of mosaic lines. See Chapter 6.

**Tessera (singular), tesserae (plural).** The word used for the individual pieces in a mosaic.

# UK MOSAIC SUPPLIERS

**For a range of tiles, tools and substrates:**
Mosaic Workshop. www.mosaicworkshop.com
Mosaic Heaven. www.mosaicheaven.com
Mosaic Supplies. www.mosaicsupplies.co.uk
Hobby Island Mosaics. www.hobby-island.co.uk

**Pebbles:**
Maggy Howarth. www.maggyhowarth.co.uk
Cedstone. www.cedstone.co.uk

**Compound Tile Nippers:**
Hobby Island Mosaics. www.hobby-island.co.uk and through Amazon.

**Hammer and Hardie:**
Xinamarie. www.xinamarie.com
Arte Marcia. www.artemarcia.com

**Substrates:**
Jackoboard. CTD Tiles. www.ctdtiles.co.uk
Wedi board. Topps Tiles. www.toppstiles.co.uk

**Glues:**
Tile Adhesive. Topps Tiles. www.toppstiles.co.uk
Weldbond Multipurpose Adhesive Glue and Titebond II Premium Wood Glue. Both are available through Amazon.

**Grout:**
Any hardware shop or tile supplier including Topps Tiles.

# ACKNOWLEDGEMENTS

Many thanks to all those who generously supplied photographs and information for this book. If you would like to see more of their work, please follow the links provided below.

Francesca Busca: www.francescabusca.com @Francesca_busca;
Martin Cheek: www.martincheek.co.uk @martincheekmosaics;
Rachel Davies: www.racheldaviesmosaics.com @racheldaviesmosaics;
Gary Drostle: www.drostle.com @garydrostle;
Rhona Duffy: www.rhonaduffymosaics.com@rhonaduffymosaics;
Tamara Froud: www.artmosaicdesign.com @mosaicallsorts;
Katy Galbraith: www.katygalbraith.co.uk @recyclememosaics;
Hackney Mosaic Project: www.hackney-mosaic.co.uk @hackneymosaicproject;
Maggy Howarth: www.maggyhowarth.co.uk @maggy_howarth_studios;
Tessa Hunkin: www.tessahunkin.co.uk @tessahunkin;
Joanna Kessel: www.joannakessel.co.uk @joannakessel;
Dugald MacInnes: www.dugaldmacinnesart.com;
Wilma van der Meyden: www.wilmavandermeyden.com @wilma_van_der_meyden;
Cleo Mussi: www.mussimosaics.co.uk @cleomussimosaics;
Helen Nock: www.helen-nock.co.uk @nockhelen;
Joy Parker: www.joyparker.org @joyaiparker;
Sue Rew: www.suerewmosaics.co.uk @suerewmosaics;
Rachel Sager: www.sagermosaics.com @sagermosaics;
John Sollinger: www.johnsollinger.com @sollinger.john;
Julie Sperling: www.sperlingmosaics.com @sperlingmosaics;
Carrie Reichardt: www.carriereichardt.com @carriereichardt;
Anabella Wewer: www.anabellawewermosaics.com, @anabellawewer.

Thanks also to the British Association for Modern Mosaic (www.bamm.org.uk @modern_mosaic) including the wonderful Scotland branch.